GREAT SEA RESCUES
VOL II

Great Sea Rescues

VOL II

By
Commander E. W. Middleton
V.R.D., R.N.V.R.

Published by Heritage Publications,
Merchants House, Barley Market Street,
Tavistock, Devon, England.

in association with

NEW ENGLISH LIBRARY
TIMES MIRROR

Commander Middleton, who wrote this book, served on the coast for many years as an inspector of lifeboats for the Royal National Lifeboat Institution and was later assistant chief inspector and superintendent of the stores and repair depot. He wishes to express his appreciation and thanks for the invaluable help he received from members of the staff of the RNLI in preparing the book and for many helpful suggestions and criticisms.

ISBN 903975–31–9

Published by Heritage Publications, Merchants House, Barley Market Street, Tavistock in association with New English Library Limited from Barnard's Inn, Holborn, London EC1N 2JR Made and printed in Great Britain by Hunt Barnard Printing Ltd., Aylesbury, Bucks.

Contents

Foreword

Writing of *Great Sea Rescues* poses the difficult question of what to leave out, rather than what to include. Anyone who has made a study of sea rescue might be forgiven for thinking that there is a dearth of outstanding material, for the same great rescues have been written and published again and again. In fact, it is not the lack of suitable stories that is responsible for the same incidents appearing in different books on the subject; it is because these particular rescues stand out for a number of reasons and also because they typify the work of rescue at sea and the dedication of the men that man the rescue craft.

Undoubtedly some fine rescues have not attracted the attention they deserve and indeed there must be many brave deeds which have gone unsung and virtually unknown. In this book some care has been taken to strike a balance between the famous and the lesser known rescues and it is hoped that this will provide a new interest and a new outlook on the drama of distress at sea.

Possibly the biggest challenge the sea rescue services have ever had to face is the enormous increase in calls for assistance from pleasure craft; due, of course, to the tremendous upsurge in sea sports. Yachts, boats, anglers, swimmers, divers have all increased in number at an astonishing rate, and since the number of accidents is almost certain to be in proportion to the number of people involved, there has also been a very great increase in the work of the coastguard, lifeboats and air/sea rescue services. There has been a great deal of criticism directed at people who put to sea without sufficient knowledge of what lies before them. But it seems possible that many of these strictures are undeserved, for in proportion to the number of people besporting themselves on, in or under the sea at any one time the casualty rate may not be thought unduly high. There may well be a good deal of beginners' luck about!

But let no one underestimate the power or unpredictability of the sea. The border line between happy, carefree sailing or swimming and sudden disaster is a very narrow one and may leave no room for second thoughts. The incidents described hereafter may perhaps serve as a warning to avoid over-confidence or carelessness in any form of sea sport.

Chapter 1

Heading for disaster

'No man will be a sailor who has contrivance enough to get himself into a jail; for being in a ship is being in a jail, with the chance of being drowned . . . ' so said Dr Samuel Johnson, a shrewd observer of the daily scene. He went on to say that a man in jail has more room, better food and commonly better company. Times have changed since the learned doctor stated his opinion of seafaring but it is still one of the most dangerous callings and every year many seamen lose their lives in disasters. Seamen have lived with disaster and danger from the beginning of time and when this fact is added to the discomfort and poor pay which was their lot until quite recently it is astonishing that men have always been found to man the ships on which the well-being of the inhabitants of Britain so largely depends.

Not only Britain but many other nations have always produced fine, hardy seamen who have a common bond in the sea and its strange attraction which draws them back voyage after voyage. Between seamen there is an understanding and a tolerance which transcends even national ties. In general, two seamen of different nations will have more in common than a seaman and a landsman of similar birth and upbringing.

In view of the importance of ships and the men who man them, for seaborne trade is vital to nearly every nation, it is strange that enormous losses of vessels and men went on for centuries before the first attempts at organised rescue were made, less than 200 years ago. There are some possible explanations for this fact but first it is necessary to consider how and why disaster at sea occurs.

When primitive man first ventured afloat, possibly on a log or bundle of reeds and quite likely inadvertantly, he would have been surprised to know that he was setting in train a whole host of problems concerned with the techniques of navigation and seamanship. If the first planned voyage was no more than the crossing of a modest stream because the grass was greener on the other side it may well have brought to light some of the effects of wind and current. Also, there was the necessity for some method of propelling a craft, however primitive, through the water at a speed sufficient to prevent it being entirely at the mercy of the elements. Any vessel may have to face a similar problem today.

Thousands of years may have passed before any attempt was made to adjust the shape of the primitive craft to make it easier to propel through the water although the problem of stability must have quickly made itself felt. Unless they had achieved the ability to swim, many pioneer navigators must have paid for their temerity by drowning. Some, more fortunate than others may have managed to reach the shore by means of their frantic splashing and realised that man could not only keep himself afloat but also propel himself along. It was undoubtedly a very valuable discovery.

So, through the centuries and the millenniums, man must have slowly and painfully learned to come to terms with the rivers and the seas. In different parts of the world, different types of craft and different techniques for handling them developed according to geographical and climatic conditions and to the uses for which the craft were required. Sails probably appeared fairly early in time, for the effect of wind on the craft itself and indeed on the bodies of the people on board must soon have been appreciated. The really important advance must have been the discovery of the ability to sail to windward, or towards the direction from which the wind was blowing. This was very probably the result of some happy accident and even today there are some different opinions as to why this is possible. After centuries of down-wind, or at best cross-wind sailing, the new discovery must have opened up all sorts of possibilities and made many more voyages possible in a given time.

The voyages down-wind made use of the prevailing winds and their seasonal changes. Indeed, even in the heyday of sail all windjammer voyages were made on the fair wind principle and their routes planned to take advantage of the trade winds, monsoons and other fairly predictable wind directions. Not only were the square-riggers poor at working to windward but they also tended to make a lot of leeway under these circumstances and might well show little progress in the desired direction after a day of hard slogging. Nevertheless, men learned to handle sailing craft with incredible skill and in the early days to overcome the host of difficulties which lack of navigational facilities and the simple resources of the time made inevitable. Some, perhaps the majority of pioneer circumnavigators commenced their incredible voyages in ships which were often leaky, cranky and ill-equipped to modern eyes. They had to be entirely self-supporting once out of home waters and capable of carrying out major repairs in any part of the world, using whatever material they could lay hands on. Sometimes long arduous journeys had to be made to get suitable spars to replace masts and yards, often in unfriendly territory.

Thus from the earliest days the seamen learned to make the best of any situation in which they found themselves and were under no illusions that they could rely on anybody else for assistance. Even so, in spite of all the difficulties and dangers of navigation without adequate charts and instruments, a clumsy, leaking ship and the worst the elements could produce, the early seamen succumbed most often to disease and injury rather than death by drowning. Not that there was any lack of opportunity to end in a watery grave as the number of ships lost round the coasts of Britain alone sometimes exceeded a thousand in a single year!

In view of the obvious possibilities of an early and inglorious end it seems incredible that men continued to go to sea for meagre wages and revolting food when there was little likelihood of fame and fortune for their trouble. There was money to be made at sea, not always legitimately, and in the days of the privateers men before the mast could and did make quick fortunes, or at least handsome sums of money; but in general seamen must have felt the call of the sea so strongly that the discomfort and danger was part of the price they were prepared to pay.

The enormous number of casualties which occurred every year were certainly not always due to lack of skill or carelessness although in many cases an ill-found ship or an incompetent master or crew undoubtedly contributed to the result. In heavy weather a sailing ship must reduce sail to ease the enormous strain which a gale force wind exerts and which could quickly bring about the loss of a mast or even cause a vessel to capsize. With sail area reduced and with the ship labouring in a heavy sea her speed would quickly drop. Indeed, it might well be necessary to heave-to with a scrap of sail just keeping the vessel more or less head to wind and sea. Under these circumstances the ship would drift slowly down wind and unless she had plenty of sea room and the nearest land many miles to leeward it would not be long before the fact that she was driving down to her doom on a storm lashed shore would become clear to all on board.

This is the classic disaster: a sailing ship unable to set sufficient sail to give control with an unfriendly shore just under her lee. It may be a ship under way on passage from port to port but it could equally well be a ship sheltering at anchor, suddenly embayed by a shift of wind.

There are many harrowing stories to illustrate the situations described and in the case of vessels at anchor the destruction has at times been wholesale and the death roll enormous. One of the worst disasters of this kind happened in November 1703 when a tremendous gale drove a fleet of 13 British ships on to the Goodwin sands off Deal and 1,200 men were reported lost. Some 200 men were said to be alive and stranded on the sands. When the mayor of Deal heard this he called on the local boatmen to try and save them but the boatmen were too busy collecting the valuable flotsam washed ashore from the wrecks and refused to help. So the mayor asked the revenue men to try and save the survivors but they too refused. Whereupon the mayor and some of the townsmen seized the revenue craft and launched them to the rescue of the stranded seamen. It would be interesting to know how successful they were and whether the brave mayor is remembered in the archives of Deal.

Like the Downs off Deal, another favourite place for ships to shelter in bad weather was Torbay. In January 1866 many ships had been sheltering there from a westerly gale but the wind moderated somewhat and a number weighed anchor and sailed. A very threatening sky caused most of them to return and by dusk there were more than seventy vessels in the bay, many of them foreign. As darkness set in the wind increased from the south-west with heavy rain and by midnight it had backed to the southward and was blowing a hurricane. The wind continued to back to the eastward and increase in violence and within a very short time 11 or 12 ships were ashore in the bay. It was intensely dark and the people on shore were unable to render any assistance except to the few survivors who were able to reach land by their own efforts. All that could be seen of the ships was the occasional flash of a lantern as the wind got round to the north-east and blew harder than ever. With so many ships in the bay and the continual backing of the wind it must have made getting under way in the dark a fearsome business but some vessels managed to do so. They must have been handled by splendid seamen.

The account of the disaster says that at dawn there was a scene of indescribable confusion. Thirty or more wrecked ships lay all round the bay with bales and barrels and splintered timber everywhere. Amongst the wreckage there were dead pigs and other animals and in some cases one vessel had driven right on top of another. Many lives were lost but an astonishing number were saved, mostly by their own exertions or by some providential happening. One young man was said to have leapt from his ship as she struck and landed on what was virtually dry ground.

Some idea of the incidence of casualties is given by the figures for the three years 1816 to 1818 when 1,100 British ships were stranded or wrecked and an average of 763 seamen lost each year. Since seamen were a vital necessity if seaborne trade were to flourish it is surprising that apparently no attempt was made to initiate an organised sea rescue service until the end of the eighteenth century.

The lack of organised rescue and to some extent any attempt at rescue at all most probably stemmed from the fact that a wreck often brought unexpected and sometimes untold wealth to the people who lived nearby. The law at one time defined a wreck as a vessel from which no creature came ashore alive and it is strongly suspected that there were cases of grisly action in the surf to ensure that this was so. As the bodies were invariably buried on the beach there was little difficulty in covering up a dreadful crime. In this the local churchmen unwittingly assisted as they refused to bury victims in consecrated ground in case they were not Christians. It is said that after a wreck had occurred poor people in the area appeared to have acquired a taste for exotic drinks like tea, cocoa and claret and the women were seen wearing dresses made from the most expensive silk. No wonder then that stories grew of ships being lured ashore by false beacons and that strong local opposition was raised to the establishment of lighthouses and other aids to navigation. Although there are suggestions that the stories of wreckers and the destruction of survivors are false or greatly exaggerated, in 1752 Parliament was sufficiently concerned in the matter to pass laws against the plundering of wrecks, preventing a survivor from trying to save his own life or putting out false lights to bring a ship into danger.

Apart from the desire for easy riches, superstition also played its part in making attempts at rescue unlikely. Many people believed it to be unlucky to save a life from the sea and that the rescuer would be made to pay for his temerity. All these suggestions must be considered in the light of the habits and conditions of the time and the fact that in many parts of the coast the inhabitants barely eked out a wretched living. Even so there are many accounts of rescues from the shore, often at considerable personal danger, so humane instincts were not entirely lacking.

In many cases willingness to attempt a rescue was not enough. Conditions might make boatwork impossible or any suitable craft might be lacking. The dangers and difficulties of shipwrecked people were common to all the coasts of Britain and abroad and a harrowing tale is told of an incident on a remote northern island. A small vessel had stranded in bad weather and her crew of six endeavoured to reach the shore by means of a rope which the local inhabitants had managed to make fast. As the survivors fought their way through the angry sea an old islander pointed out that their supplies for the winter were barely sufficient to feed themselves and asked how they were to support the additional mouths, as there was no hope of getting more food. At this a young man raised his axe and cut the hawser at a blow, dashing the wretched sailors into the boiling surf between the rocks.

In spite of the purely local benefits arising from a wreck on a nearby shore the loss of trained seamen, if not of the ships themselves, must have had a serious effect on the country's seaborne trade. At the time the only efficient and inexpensive way to move goods in bulk was by sea. Roads were little more than dirt tracks and the cost of cartage over long distances prohibitive. Coal became the main item of merchandise and great fleets of colliers were employed in moving ever increasing quantities to London and the south from Newcastle and other ports. Colliers were sturdy vessels and considered to provide prime training for seamen. A shining example of collier-trained seamen was Captain James Cook, whose faith in these vessels was such that he used them for each of his explorations.

It was not until towards the end of the eighteenth century that the first records of the establishment of a coast rescue service appear. In 1772 Dr John Sharp, Archdeacon of Northumberland, succeeded to the living of Bamburgh and control of a trust which supported a number of charities. These were administered from Bamburgh castle which stood starkly on a headland overlooking the Farne islands with Holy island and Lindisfarne a few miles away. Many vessels were wrecked on this rugged stretch of coastline and Dr Sharp was greatly distressed at the plight of the survivors. He took efficient steps to alleviate their sufferings and provided accommodation for them in the castle. By establishing a system of coast look-outs and signals he endeavoured to bring help to vessels in distress as promptly as possible. Later he approached Lionel Lukin, one of the three men credited with having invented the lifeboat, and asked him to modify a local boat known as a coble for use in rescue work. This would appear to be the first sea rescue service of which there is a record.

In spite of the stories of deliberate wrecking, the plundering of wrecks and the destruction of survivors, there is also no doubt that rescues were carried out from the earliest times. Many survivors owed their lives to the efforts of the crews of pilot cutters, revenue cutters and naval vessels. Captain Marryat, who wrote so many stirring sea stories, was himself responsible for saving more than one person from drowning. Pilot cutters kept to sea in all weathers on the look-out for homeward bound ships and to take pilots off outward bound vessels when clear of pilotage waters. They were fine, sturdy vessels, superbly handled and there was fierce competition between the various cutters to be first alongside a vessel and put their man on board. In the Bristol channel this once led to a complaint that the cutters had become a danger to other vessels but the pilots claimed that the contrary was the case. One said he had saved four ship's crews in his cutter and that in a heavy gale of wind he stood by two small craft for 23 hours and saved the crews. Rescues were also carried out by individuals on the spot, as in the case of a French vessel trying to make the shelter of Dover harbour in a strong gale and heavy sea. She was dashed against the harbour wall and broke up, but some of her crew managed to scramble on to some wreckage. On shore, four sailors saw their plight and launched a boat from the beach and picked them up safely but the boat capsized and rescuers and rescued all drifted ashore together.

The advent of steam propulsion did not at once remove the inherent danger of the lee shore and in fact produced some new elements of disaster. Engines were crude but fairly reliable; it was the boilers which gave trouble in spite of the fact that steam pressures of only a few pounds per square inch were all that they were expected to produce. A classic case of an early steamship disaster was that of the *Forfarshire*, now principally remembered for the part played by Grace Darling in the rescue of the survivors.

The paddle-steamer *Forfarshire* of 300 tons had sailed from Hull on 5 September 1838 with a number of passengers and a crew of 23. She was bound for Dundee and carried a general cargo. One of her boilers had been leaking and temporary repairs had been carried out while the ship lay at Hull. Next day off Flamborough head trouble developed in another boiler, from which boiling water was leaking all over the stokehold, so the engineer decided to draw fires. The weather worsened and the ship was able to make little headway against a strong north-west wind. Soon the wind veered to the east of north, putting the ship on a lee shore just as it had been decided to set her auxiliary sails. At the same time the engines failed completely.

It is not difficult to imagine the scene in the stokehold of the doomed vessel. As attempts were made to continue firing the boilers, escaping steam and the glare of the furnaces must have given a fair imitation of an inferno, with scalding hot water from the leaks sluicing across the iron decks with every violent roll and pitch of the ship. Yet the men below must have been dedicated believers in the power and ability of their primitive machinery and loath to accept the fact that natural forces were about to destroy them.

During the night the ship was driven further and further south until at last a flashing light was sighted. This the captain took to be the Inner Farne light and he is said to have decided to steer inshore in order to obtain some shelter from the Farne islands themselves but in fact the ship must have been virtually out of control. The light they had sighted was actually that of the Longstone, some distance north-east of the Inner Farne. Shortly afterwards the ship struck a rock called the Big Harcar and almost immediately split in two, the after end breaking up in the waves and carrying many people swiftly to their death. The master of the *Forfarshire*, Captain Humble, and his wife were swept overboard together leaving 13 survivors on board, including a woman and two children. By morning the two children were dead from exposure and only their mother and eight men were still alive.

The keeper of the Longstone lighthouse was William Darling who lived there with his family. On the night of the disaster his wife and daughter Grace, who was 22 years of age, were in the lighthouse with him. It was Grace who first sighted the wreck in the early morning and it was some time before her father was able to confirm that there were any survivors.

Father and daughter launched the lighthouse boat, a coble, and as it was too big for Darling to handle on his own, Grace, who no doubt well knew how to handle an oar, went with him. The rock on which the survivors now were was only a few hundred yards away in a direct line but in order to reach it safely they had to pull for nearly a mile.

When they reached the rock and discovered how many survivors there were it was clear that two trips would be necessary in order to get them all to the lighthouse. On the first journey Darling took the mother, deeply shocked at the loss of her two children, an injured man and two others. With these two he then returned to the rock and brought back the remaining survivors. Not long after all were safely in the lighthouse the North Sunderland lifeboat, which had managed to launch in spite of the adverse conditions, arrived on the scene but of course too late to render assistance.

It was some time before the part played by the Darlings became generally known. To begin with, people were much too concerned at the loss of what was considered a fine steamer and the consequent death roll, but gradually the news filtered through. *The Times* summed up the situation with the sentence 'Is there in the whole field of history or of fiction, even one instance of female heroism to compare for one moment with this?'

Grace, and to a lesser extent her father became national heroes and a very great number of people and organisations went to considerable lengths to cash in on the enthusiasm of the public. But Grace, who behaved throughout all the adulation with becoming modesty did not live long to enjoy her fame. She survived the incident a brief four years to die at the age of 26.

It is easy to understand how the early steamships got into difficulties, handicapped as they were by the low power of their engines and the doubtful value of their auxiliary sails in an emergency. But the improvement in steamship design and technique by no means checked the casualty rate entirely and many fine steamships – and later, motorships – have found ways of hurrying to disaster. A fairly recent example was the loss of the *Samtampa* in the Bristol channel in April 1947 when the Mumbles lifeboat, launched to her assistance, was lost with all hands. When day dawned, the wrecked ship lay broken in three parts at Sker point on the Glamorgan coast. Not far away on the jagged rocks lay the upturned lifeboat.

The *Samtampa*, bound for Newport in ballast, had a crew of 41 men. She had experienced difficulty in steering on her way up the Bristol channel because of her light draught and a gale force wind on her starboard quarter. Approaching Nash point and only about 40 miles from her destination she became completely out of control and her master decided to anchor in the hope of riding out the storm. To continue would have meant that the wind and waves would have inevitably have driven the vessel ashore, for the land was now close under her lee. With both anchors down the *Samtampa* was clearly dragging and her master made urgent radio calls for assistance saying that he was doubtful whether he could prevent the ship from grounding. His assessment of the situation was only too accurate and at 1900 that evening his ship struck the rocks of Sker point and broke up almost at once. The coastguard were on the scene with their life-saving apparatus but the most powerful rockets failed to reach the ship against the now hurricane force wind. Even had a connection been made it is doubtful whether it would have been possible to get men through the surf and over the rocky ledge alive.

Messages from the *Samtampa* indicating the gravity of her situation had been received by Burnham radio and passed to the coastguard at Mumbles who requested the lifeboat to launch. At 1810 that evening the 45ft Watson type lifeboat

Edward, Prince of Wales, launched from the boathouse by Mumbles pier with Coxswain William Gammon and a crew of seven. The weather was extremely bad with fierce squalls and a very high, breaking sea. Visibility was poor and the prospect of an attempt to take men off a large steamer aground on a rocky lee shore must have been daunting, even to the hardy, experienced William Gammon and his men. Just after the boat left the slipway some further information was received by telephone so she was recalled. Having received the new instructions the gallant crew waved acknowledgement as the lifeboat plunged away on her 12 mile journey to Sker point on the other side of Mumbles bay. Daylight was fast fading. The crew were never seen alive again.

From the time she left Mumbles there was no further communication with the lifeboat but as she was not fitted with radio the only possibility of news would have been from a sighting or signals by morse lamp. At Sker point, car headlights provided sparse illumination for the last scenes of the tragedy as the onlookers watched helplessly. At 0200 the tide had fallen sufficiently for a police officer to make his way across the rocks to the after part of the wreck but he found no one. At daybreak the lifeboat was found on the rocks bottom up and during the day the bodies of her crew of eight were found. Some were close to the boat and others on a sandy beach nearby. Three of them had head injuries and all were wearing lifebelts, properly secured.

A bare two hundred yards away from the lifeboat the forward and after sections of the *Samtampa* lay alongside one another, high and dry, with bow and stern together inshore. The middle section containing the bridge and engine-room had sunk in deep water just clear of the rocky ledge. It was clear that all the crew had gathered on the bridge superstructure as being the highest part of the ship and as a result every one of the crew of 41 had lost their lives. All the bodies when recovered were black with fuel oil from the bunker tanks of the *Samtampa*. The melancholy task of cleaning them was carried out in a nearby factory where cleaning fluid was available and the bodies were then laid out in a temporary mortuary which had once served as a gunnery training dome.

How the *Samtampa* had met her end was clearly evident. One anchor cable had parted under the strain of bringing the ship up and the other anchor had dragged until the ship struck. Alas, the hull broke into three pieces and the mid-ship section, which contained the engines, apparently sank like a stone, carrying the whole of the crew with it. In the bow and stern sections on shore the living spaces were free of water and the bedding in the fo'c'sle bone dry. It is reasonably certain that any men who might have stayed in these parts of the ship would have been saved but it would have needed an iron nerve and considerable foresight to do so. It may also be deduced that had the ship not been of welded construction the story might have had a different ending.

The final events which led to the loss of the lifeboat and her brave crew are entirely a matter of conjecture but certain possibilities may be taken as being likely to have happened. When the lifeboat arrived in the vicinity of the wreck the shore was probably a mass of lights from onlookers' cars and those of the rescue parties. From seaward it may well have been difficult to assess the situation but the *Samtampa* must have already broken up. It would seem that sometime about high water, with the storm still at its height, Coxswain Gammon decided to close the wreck in a rescue attempt. Close inshore the lifeboat must have been capsized by a huge breaker, made more dangerous by the backwash from Sker point itself. On a dead lee shore with a steep rocky ledge the main break of the sea must have been terrifying and the lifeboat overwhelmed before the crew could make a move of any sort.

So 49 men died, swiftly and inexorably, and the sea had once more proved itself the master. Whether the disaster should have happened was discussed at length at the time and could still be debated. Once more a lifeboat crew had shown their willingness to take any risks to try and save the lives of seamen and had paid for this with their own lives. The RNLI as is its usual practice granted pensions to all their dependants and a fund opened by the mayor of Swansea reached the sum of £91,000. The new lifeboat which replaced the one lost was named the *William Gammon*.

The loss of ships and men already described have been due principally to bad weather but faulty navigation and seamanship have been responsible for a large proportion of casualties and in spite of the effective aids of the electronic age still continue to do so. Indeed, the electronic age has produced its own particular problems, one of which is the 'radar assisted collision' of which there have been many examples.

One of the more spectacular examples of disaster due to faulty navigation was that of the *Torrey Canyon*, wrecked on the Seven Stones reef in broad daylight with easily recognisable landmarks in sight. From a rescue point of view the wreck did not present any problems but the 118,000 tons of oil which was her cargo most certainly did.

Chapter 2

Rescues past and present

A RESCUE LONG AGO: It may be unwise to speak of 'long ago', for people live to great ages and memories seem to work better in the long past than in the immediate present. Certainly one may still find old, but seemingly hale and hearty seamen who can speak convincingly of some happening it is certain they cannot have actually witnessed. But here by long past is meant an event that happened nearly two hundred years ago. Over such a long period of time it would be fussy to be too precise.

As an example of what one may achieve it would be difficult to better a rescue which took place at Plymouth as long ago as January 1796. The hero of this exploit was no less a person than Sir Edward Pellew, a captain in the Royal Navy who served with Lord Nelson and for whom he had great admiration and affection. Few of the naval captains of that time commanded so much admiration and respect as Edward Pellew and there is every reason to believe that he was not only extremely pleasant but a most outstanding man in every way.

A ship of the line, HMS *Indefatigable* was at anchor in the Hamoaze at Plymouth and her captain, Sir Edward Pellew, was driving with Lady Pellew to dine with a friend, Dr Hawker. On the way they saw people running towards the Hoe and asked the reason for all the excitement. The answer was that the *Dutton*, a large East Indiaman, had put into Plymouth to shelter from the gales raging in the Channel and on being moved to a berth in the Cattewater had struck a shoal and lost her rudder. Out of control she had swept across to the other side of the channel and grounded on the rocks below the citadel.

On learning of the accident Sir Edward jumped from the

carriage and joined the hurrying throng to a point where the *Dutton* could be seen. (What happened to Lady Pellew and her dinner is not recorded.)

When Sir Edward came in sight of the Indiaman she was fast on the rocks, broadside on and rolling heavily in the waves. The gale which had made her seek shelter was increasing in violence and as the stricken vessel rolled her mainmast came crashing down, adding to the confusion on board. It was clear that all the people in the ship, and there were several hundred of them, were in grave danger, for anyone in the water would certainly be drowned or beaten to death on the rocky shore.

Sir Edward tried to persuade pilots and watermen to take their boats off to the ship but none would do so. But there was a rope from the ship to the shore by which the officers were said to have deserted her, though how this was got across is not reported. Sir Edward plunged into the surf and by means of the rope pulled himself off to the wreck and was hauled aboard by members of the crew. In doing so they dragged him under the fallen mainmast, hurting his back, but at the time he ignored the injury and set to work to restore order and discipline. His name and fame were so well known that there were cheers when he told them who he was. He told those on board that they would all be saved if they obeyed his orders and he assured them that he would be the last to leave the ship. Soon he had managed to get more hawsers ashore, using the original rope to haul them across, with the help of willing hands on the beach. Then boats from his own ship, to which he had sent instructions, began to arrive and women and children were taken ashore in them rather than subject them to the hazardous journey by rope through the surf. Sir Edward improvised cradles which were hauled along the ropes in similar fashion to the breeches buoy used by the coastguard today. The ropes on which the cradles were slung were kept taut by men tending them as the ship rolled, hauling away as they became slack and easing them as the weight of the ship came on them. The whole operation must have taken a considerable time and it says much for the organising ability and clear thinking of Sir Edward Pellew. There is no doubt that in the days of sail a competent seaman simply had to be quick, resourceful and courageous if he were to survive the rigours of his calling. Strict discipline was also essential and a great deal of the harsh treatment of seamen, of which so much has been written, was probably necessary for the safety and well-being of all on board. Once discipline was relaxed, even to the slightest hesitation in obeying an order, the ship might well be in danger.

On this occasion, as with many other wrecks, some of the survivors sought courage or consolation with the contents of the spirit-room. The account says that these men were soldiers but there were probably others involved. It was also reported that Sir Edward again restored order at the point of his drawn sword but it is difficult to imagine him going out to the ship, hand over hand along the rope through the surf, with a sword at his side. Perhaps the sword belonged to one of the drunken soldiers!

Sir Edward kept his word and was the last person to leave the ship. He modestly recorded the event in his journal by writing 'Sent two boats to the assistance of a ship on shore in the sound.' His own part in the rescue had been seen and appreciated, however, and he was voted the freedom of the town by the Plymouth corporation.

The Royal Navy itself was by no means free from the perils of shipwreck and a book entitled 'Shipwrecks of the Royal Navy', published in 1864 lists no fewer than 422 casualties between 1793 and 1857, an average of more than six a year. It must be admitted that some were very small craft and some managed to get listed as wrecks on several occasions, so were obviously not total losses.

An interesting example of the difficulties of maintaining an accurate position by dead reckoning in the days of sail is shown in the story of the *Pallas* and the *Nymph.* In the month of December 1810 the *Pallas*, a 32-gun frigate commanded by Captain Paris Monke, was returning from a month's cruise on the coast of Norway in company with the *Nymph*, Captain Edward Sneyd Clay, and was steering for Leith with a prize in tow. Land was discovered on Tuesday 18 December but the weather was thick and it could not be identified. Later in the day they fell in with some fishermen who said the ship was off Stonehive and the Tod head. The pilot made several alterations of course and as night approached, with the wind increasing, sail was shortened. Presently a light was sighted which the pilot insisted was on the pier at Arbroath, whereupon the captain asked if they should not therefore be in sight of the Bell rock. The pilot replied that they should soon see it and orders were given for a sharp look-out to be kept.

Not long afterwards the officer of the watch went below to report to the captain that May island light was in sight and Captain Monke was in the act of going on deck when the ship struck. He instantly rushed on deck and asked the master where he supposed the ship had grounded. He replied that he was afraid that they were on the Bell rock and continued, '. . . and not a soul will be saved unless we can forge her over it'. How they could possibly be on the Bell rock when the master had so confidently declared that they were running from it for some hours remains a mystery but there was no time to argue. Captain Monke ordered the drum to beat to quarters and the men were soon on deck and each at his post. The yards were braced up and the lead was cast, showing a depth of twelve feet. The ship now began to strike the ground with great violence and when they found she would not forge ahead the yards were braced aback but she still remained hard and fast.

Land was now seen to leeward and the master changed his opinion and imagined that the frigate had struck on the Isle of May but the pilot thought they were in St Andrew's bay and blamed the master for having hauled too soon.

Orders were given to man the pumps which was done with alacrity, the work going on throughout the night. As the moon rose it became clear that the vessel was close to the land, her bow a short distance from the nearest rocks. Voices were heard but it was impossible to make out the words. The *Pallas* became more and more uneasy; her rudder was carried away and the seas broke right over her. In order to lighten the vessel the mainmast was cut away. The foremast followed and the mizen was to be next but the axes were lost or washed away. The ship by this time was on her beam ends with the sea making breaches over her, so that every individual had enough to do to keep himself from being washed overboard.

Many of the men by this time were suffering much from cold, hunger and fatigue and those who were able got into the weather chains for safety and shelter. At daylight they discovered the real position of the ship; it was evident from their bearings that the frigate was on shore near Dunbar, about 13 miles to the southward of the Isle of May, having overrun her distance by some three hours. She was now a total wreck; much of the bottom had separated from the upperworks and the iron ballast in the hold was open to view. It was now time for every man to provide as far as possible for his own safety. A Portuguese sailor was the first to quit the wreck and swim ashore and several men attempted to follow him but five of them perished. The lifeboat from Dunbar, which had been launched with great difficulty owing to the high surf, reached the ship at ten o'clock in the morning and took off a boat-load of survivors, landing them safely.

All the boats of the *Pallas* were stove, or otherwise useless, with the exception of the cutter which was now launched and reached the land with as many as she could carry. The lifeboat made a second successful trip but at her third attempt when filled with people she capsized. In this accident six of the crew of the *Pallas* were drowned and one of the bravest fellows from the lifeboat. The rest were saved by the efforts of the crew of a small fishing boat. This same boat persevered with efforts to save the rest of the frigate's crew by running a line from the ship to the shore. Along this line the boat was hauled back and forth from the wreck eight or ten times until the remaining men were safe ashore. With the exception of some ten or twelve men the whole of the ship's company was saved. Once on shore the survivors were well looked after and it was said that the kindness and hospitality of the inhabitants of Dunbar and the surrounding country were beyond all praise.

The *Nymph*, which was in company with the *Pallas*, went ashore the same night on a rock called the Devil's Ark, near Skethard. The crew were all saved but the frigate was lost.

The island of Anglesey is not often in the news but it has a splendid seafaring tradition and as is mentioned elsewhere in this book, the Anglesey lifeboats have a record of brilliant rescues which few places can equal. Two names which stand out in the history of the Anglesey lifeboats are those of James and Frances Williams. It is said that on the day they arrived at their new home in Anglesey the Williams' saw the sailing packet *Alert* lost after striking the West Mouse rock, when she sank immediately drowning 140 people. From that moment onward the Williams devoted much of their time to the cause of life-saving at sea and were largely responsible for the provision and maintenance of lifeboats on the Anglesey coast. And at that time there was a great deal of local shipping apart from that bound for the Mersey. In his fascinating book 'Ships and seamen of Anglesey' Aled Eames points out that James Williams was no 'Boffin' but took an active part in the work of rescue. He quotes an interesting example:

On 7 March 1835 the smack *Active* of Belfast was attempting to enter the little harbour of Cemais but grounded a long way from shore, every wave making a complete breach over her. Boats had been launched to her assistance but had failed to get through the surf but James Williams, who had ridden over from his home when he heard of the casualty, took charge on the spot. In order to get a line out to the smack he swam his horse out to her and threw a grapnel into the bowsprit shrouds. Using the line he attached, a boat was hauled out to her and her crew of five was found huddled in the cabin, too exhausted to help themselves so that they had to be assisted to safety. Later the same year when the ship *Sarah* was driven on to the rocks near Trecastell, Williams 'happened to be in the neighbourhood' and once again took charge of the rescue operations. This time also, a line was got from the ship to the shore and 14 men safely landed. On another occasion, when one of the lighthouse keepers on the Skerries was taken ill and needed medical attention, Frances Williams took her medicine chest and went out with her husband in the lifeboat and tended the sick man. These brief notes do less than justice to the work of rescue on the coast of Anglesey in the times mentioned but at least may help to show the background of the gold medals won in more recent days.

And now, a rather large jump in time takes us across the Irish sea to County Down in Northern Ireland where at 0045 on 21 January 1942 the coastguard informed the Cloughey lifeboat station that a steamer was ashore half a mile off Ballyquinton. At 0140 the lifeboat *Herbert John* launched into a south-east gale with a very heavy sea and sleet and rain. It was a wild night indeed. Just before the launch another message was received warning the coxswain that the vessel had struck on a very rocky part of the coast and that the coastguard breeches buoy apparatus was on its way to the spot. The lifeboat reached the casualty at 0330 and found her high and dry on the rocks, making it impossible to reach her from seaward. At this time, with the ship high and dry, the crew were quite safe.

The coxswain decided to stand by the ship as with the rising tide the situation might alter and make it necessary to take the crew off the steamer but at this moment ships were sighted to the northward, apparently off course and heading for the shore. The lifeboat immediately made for the ships, which were part of a convoy, but on reaching them found that several had already gone ashore and two others were about to strike. A warning was flashed by lamp and a destroyer, which was also heading towards the shore, fired a star shell which illuminated the lifeboat. The destroyer then turned and headed seawards, no doubt to warn the rest of the convoy.

Seven vessels had gone ashore, a grim reminder that in wartime at sea all the dangers are not those provided by the enemy. The absence of warning lights from lighthouses and buoys and the fact that all ships were darkened presented an additional hazard to navigators particularly in thick weather. The seven vessels were all so far in shore that the lifeboat could not get near enough to render any useful assistance, so she lay off until daylight. She then went to each ship in turn but with the exception of one they were all so firmly aground that the crews were in no danger. The one ship which was in enough depth of water for the lifeboat to get alongside was the *Orminster*, of London, and she had 68 people on board. Her master asked the lifeboat to stand by as he thought he might get the ship off at high water and he asked the coxswain to pilot him out of the maze of rocks. The coxswain agreed to do this but the ship defied all efforts to refloat her and some of the crew were taken off by the lifeboat. Later they were instructed to return to the ship by the captain and as none of the crews of the stranded ships were in danger the lifeboat returned to Cloughey.

Soon after the Cloughey lifeboat had launched the coastguard informed the Newcastle, Co. Down, station of the fact, it being the usual practice to inform the adjacent stations when a lifeboat launches. The Newcastle crew assembled and some three hours later the coastguard informed them that four ships had gone ashore off Ballyquinton. On this it was decided to launch and at five o'clock in the morning the lifeboat *L.P. and St Helen* left harbour. She had over 20 miles to go to the position off Ballyquinton and there was now a strong south-east gale, a high sea and sleet squalls. It was still very dark and at times the coxswain could barely see a boat's length ahead.

The Newcastle lifeboat had to cross Strangford bar where a nine knot current was running out against the gale, causing a welter of breaking sea, running in all directions. Coxswain Patrick Murphy had to nurse his boat through this turbulent race, heading out to sea with the current for a distance of nearly six miles before he could turn and make his way back towards the land. It was then necessary to stream the drogue, a big canvas cone, towed astern to prevent a boat broaching-to when running with a following sea.

At 1030 the Newcastle boat arrived at the stranded ships and found not four, but seven of them ashore. One, the *Browning* of Liverpool, was further out than the rest with her after end fast on a reef of rocks. When asked earlier by the Cloughey coxswain if he needed assistance her captain had said that he did not wish the crew to be taken off. Since then the coastguard had got 17 men ashore with their breeches buoy apparatus leaving 39 men still on board. But the rising tide had driven the coastguard rescue team off the rocky shore and made it impossible for more survivors to be taken off this way.

On board the *Browning* was a number of bloodstock stallions which had gone wild with fear and broken loose. The captain had given orders for them to be shot as they had become a very real danger but in the confusion the man who did it put two bullets through his own hand. The situation on board almost defies description with the ship on a reef, a howling gale blowing and a number of stallions wild with fear, charging about on the narrow decks. Dr Samuel Johnson would no doubt have made an even more trenchant comment on the life of a sailor had he known of anything like this.

This was the position when the Newcastle lifeboat arrived. Coxswain Murphy anchored to windward of the ship and commenced to veer down towards her. Now the seas were breaking right over the casualty and at one moment the lifeboat was lifted as high as the steamer's rails, only her anchor warp preventing her landing right on the *Browning*'s deck. Next moment the backwash caught hold of the lifeboat and whirled her away. Murphy made three attempts, anchoring in a different place each time but after an hour it was clear that it was impossible to effect a rescue from the windward side.

As the vessel lay there seemed little prospect of an approach to leeward as her bow was very close to the rocks. Murphy hailed the ship's captain and asked if he thought there was water for the lifeboat to leeward and the reply was 'Yes, but not much'. In fact the gap between the steamer's bow and the rocks was barely twice the beam of the lifeboat so it left very little room for error. Murphy did not hesitate and took his boat through the narrow gap, sliding through on the top of a breaker as his crew held their breath or shut their eyes. Once through the lifeboat was in a little lagoon of comparatively smooth water, protected by the towering hull of the ship itself.

Twenty-nine of the crew of the *Browning* boarded the lifeboat safely – one person more than she was designed to carry in rough weather. This left ten men still on board the casualty and although this meant a heavily overloaded boat which was already in a difficult position from which to escape Murphy realised that he could not leave the remaining men on board and shouted to them to join the lifeboat. Many of the survivors were exhausted and there was little comfort for them in the lifeboat but there were no complaints.

Now came the problem of how to get the over-loaded boat out of the lagoon. There was no room to turn and no possibility of negotiating the narrow gap through which they had come, stern first. This left nothing for it but to go out round the stern of the vessel, which was fast on the rocks. Just how much water there was there was in some doubt and it meant going out on the top of a wave, as they had come in, in order to ensure the maximum amount of water under the keel of the lifeboat. It was an extremely hazardous undertaking as if the boat touched the rocks she would almost certainly capsize leaving rescuers and rescued with little chance of survival.

Murphy knew the risks and also knew he had no choice. Choosing his time well, as three big seas rolled in one after the other, he called for full speed ahead – 'Give her all she's got!' – and the lifeboat gallantly swept over the rocks, round the stern of the *Browning* to the comparative safety of the gale wracked open sea. None of the survivors realised what was going to happen but when the mate of the *Browning* saw what had been done he said he would never have left his ship had he known such a chance must be taken.

There were still problems. Newcastle was 20 miles away and with the small freeboard of the heavily over-loaded boat a journey of that length into the teeth of the gale would have been nearly impossible. So they headed away to the north, through unfamiliar waters, the drogue streamed to offset the danger of broaching in the high, following sea. Many of the survivors must have wondered what was going to happen next and possibly felt that they might have done better to take their chance on board their own ship.

At two-thirty in the afternoon, nine hours after setting out from Newcastle, Murphy brought the lifeboat safely into the little harbour of Portavogie. Here the survivors were landed, six of them being taken at once to hospital. The crew of the lifeboat, themselves wet, cold and exhausted, went home by road, arriving at ten-thirty that night. Two days later they returned to Portavogie and sailed the lifeboat home again.

In the official report of the service it was said that the coxswain showed daring, coolness and superb seamanship. He was awarded the RNLI gold medal and later the British Empire Medal. Robert Agnew, the motor mechanic, received the silver medal and the remaining members of the crew, the bronze medal.

As a matter of interest, the ordinary scale award in cash for this long and arduous service was at that time £1.8.6 (£1.42½) but this was increased by the RNLI making an additional payment of £5 a man.

The loss of the *Princess Victoria*: It is fortunately rare nowadays for a passenger vessel to get into difficulties and for passengers to lose their lives as a result of a sea disaster. One of the most unexpected and unusual maritime casualties on the coast of Britain occurred in January 1953. Not only was the ship involved nearly new but with all modern equipment and methods available to the rescue services she could not be found when she asked for assistance. And this was apparently only a few miles from land, not long after leaving her home port.

At 0745 on 31 January 1953 the British Motorship *Princess Victoria* left Stranraer on her normal ferry trip to Larne in Northern Ireland, a distance of some 30 miles of open sea. On board were 127 passengers, a crew of 49 and a number of motor cars and other vehicles. The *Princess Victoria* was built as a car ferry and was fitted with stern doors through which vehicles were embarked.

From Stranraer the course lay northwards out of Loch Ryan and as soon as she reached the open sea she met heavy weather. A severe north-westerly gale was blowing with frequent squalls of sleet and snow and visibility varying from practically nil to three or four miles.

Soon after the ship met the heavy weather a big sea burst open the stern doors to the car deck and stove in the starboard section, also buckling some stanchions. This prevented the doors being properly closed again and a succession of heavy seas completed the damage, leaving both doors almost wide open so that water rushed in and flooded the car deck.

Portpatrick radio station received a message, not an SOS, from the *Princess Victoria* at 0946. It said 'Hove-to off mouth of Loch Ryan. Vessel not under command. Urgent assistance of tug required.' An hour later an SOS asking for immediate help was received by the Portpatrick lifeboat station and at 1100 the lifeboat *Jeanie Speirs* was launched.

The position given in the SOS was four miles north-west of Corsewall point, which lies about three miles west of the entrance to Loch Ryan. The lifeboat accordingly made for the position given, the wind now gusting up to hurricane force and setting up a high, confused sea. Conditions could hardly have been worse and the lifeboat had a very unpleasant journey north from her station.

On arrival at the reported position there was nothing to be seen and as the wind had now veered to the north Coxswain McConnell began to search to the southward as being the most probable direction of drift of the disabled ship.

At 1252 the *Princess Victoria* sent a message to both Portpatrick radio station and the destroyer HMS *Contest* which by then was also searching for her. This message said that her condition was critical and that the starboard engine-room was flooded. Quarter of an hour later she reported that she was stopped and on her beam ends, followed quickly by the ominous message 'We are preparing to abandon ship.'

The plight of the passengers can well be imagined. Within minutes of meeting the full force of the storm in the open sea, this fine modern ferry had become an unmanageable, water-logged and listing wreck. And as time went on, more and more water poured aboard, increasing the list and making movement about the ship almost impossible. At first, everyone must have thought that as the accident happened so close to the mouth of Loch Ryan and so soon after sailing, help must be near at hand. How wrong they were! Later it must have dawned on every person on board that unless help did arrive very soon the ship, her crew and her passengers had little hope of surviving.

In fact, the *Princess Victoria* sank shortly after two o'clock that afternoon, about six hours after sailing from Stranraer. Her need of assistance had been known for more than four hours but nobody had been able to find her. No calculations of the effect of wind and tide, no radio bearings, no radar had been able to give a reasonably accurate estimate of her position apparently. But at 1530, an hour and a half after the ferry sank, the Portpatrick lifeboat after a long search in appalling conditions, actually sighted wreckage. Shortly afterwards two survivors were seen on rafts and taken aboard the lifeboat.

When the message was received from the master of the *Princess Victoria* that they were preparing to abandon ship the Bangor, Co. Down coastguard informed the Donaghadee lifeboat station and said that the Portpatrick lifeboat had gone to her assistance. He also gave the estimated position of the casualty as somewhere between Belfast and Portpatrick, which must have set the Donaghadee coxswain something of a problem, particularly in view of the extremely bad weather and poor visibility. Nevertheless the Donaghadee lifeboat *Samuel Kelly* launched at 1340, which was fortunate as at 1402 the coastguard informed the coxswain by radio that the *Princess Victoria* was six miles north-east of Mew island, which lies at the entrance to Belfast lough. It meant that the casualty had drifted right across the North channel and some 24 miles to the southward. The position given was shortly afterwards amended to five miles east of the Copeland islands, further south still.

Having arrived at the last position given, which was only seven or eight miles from her station, the Donaghadee boat found no trace of the ship or survivors but did sight the destroyer *Contest* which was making all speed to the south-south-east. This again proved to be a false clue for not long afterwards Coxswain Hugh Nelson received a message from a merchant ship, the SS *Orchy* that she was approaching survivors in a position four miles north-east of Mew island. He altered course at once and soon after three o'clock the *Samuel Kelly* reached the scene of the disaster. She rescued 29 people from a ship's lifeboat, one from a raft and one from another ship's lifeboat. She continued to search until five o'clock but found no other survivors and in view of the condition of those she had picked up set course for Donaghadee. A lifeboat is not noted for comfort at the best of times but for the 31 survivors the two hour search in appalling weather conditions must have made considerable demands on their stamina and morale. Although no doubt after their previous experience to be in a lifeboat at all was a distinct relief.

The Cloughey lifeboat, stationed fifteen miles south of Donaghadee, also launched at half past two having been informed of the situation by the Tara coastguard. She made her way north, plunging into the worst of the gale, and searched until six o'clock but found nothing. She contacted the Portpatrick lifeboat which was still on the scene and piloted her into Donaghadee where they arrived at half past seven.

The Newcastle, Co. Down, lifeboat *William and Laura* also launched at 1620 at the request of the Kilkeen coastguard but she, too, found nothing and returned to her station at 2230.

The work of the Donaghadee lifeboat had not been completed when she landed her 31 survivors. At nine-thirty that night Bangor coastguard reported that the trawler *Eastcotes* had one survivor and six bodies on board. She was anchored in Belfast lough. At 2145 the *Samuel Kelly* launched once more to find the gale still blowing and conditions little better. Coxswain Nelson asked the skipper of the *Eastcotes* to weigh anchor and proceed to a more sheltered position on the Antrim coast. Here the lifeboat took from her the one survivor and six bodies, also seven bags of mail that had been picked up from the sea. She then returned to Donaghadee which she reached early on the morning of 1 February. At seven o'clock the same morning she set out again to search once more for survivors, now with better weather and visibility and with the help of aircraft. She searched until dark during which time twelve bodies and three bags of mail were recovered. She arrived back at her station at seven-thirty that evening.

It is no exaggeration to say that the whole country was horrified at the suddenness and magnitude of the disaster. That a well-found, modern ship could be so quickly overwhelmed in home waters, close to her terminal port seemed inexplicable and the difficulty in finding the casualty only added to the puzzle.

How did the stern doors become damaged to such an extent with the ship, presumably, head to sea? Was there some other factor involved? In spite of the precise and lengthy official enquiry there still seems to be something missing to account for a disaster in which, out of a total of 176 people on board, only 31 survived.

The subsequent recognition of these long and arduous services in the worst of weather conditions throws an interesting light on the evaluation system employed by the RNLI. Coxswain Hugh Nelson of Donaghadee and Coxswain William McConnell of Portpatrick were both awarded the bronze medal for the courage, skill and initiative they showed. The motor mechanics of the two lifeboats were awarded the Thanks of the Institution inscribed on vellum. From this it is clear that the grade of medal awarded is chosen according to the element of risk and skill involved in the actual rescue, without a great deal of consideration for the hardships undergone or the time afloat. In other words a brilliant and extremely dangerous rescue might win a gold medal in a matter of minutes whereas, in the case of the *Princess Victoria*, many hours of search and battling away in high seas but picking up survivors from their boats or rafts demanded no more than the bronze medal. When a lifeboatman is seen wearing an RNLI medal it may be taken for granted that he did not win it easily.

A nick of time rescue: Winter is long and hard in the Shetland isles and with the sea close on every doorstep the hardy inhabitants have little to learn of gale conditions. Even in the many inlets and voes, sheltered as they may look on a map, the winter gales come screaming in and thrash the water into foam. So when a Shetland lifeboat gets a call and a gale is blowing her crew will have no illusions about what they have to face, although they probably accept it philosophically, with the calm confidence of true seamen.

One such occasion was on the afternoon of 26 December 1956 when the honorary secretary of the Lerwick lifeboat station received a message from the coastguard saying that the Swedish motor vessel *Samba* had broken down and was drifting 122 miles south-east of Lerwick. A moderate south-east gale was blowing and a trawler was standing by the disabled ship. With the position of the casualty so far away it was not suggested that the Lerwick lifeboat should launch at this stage.

Next afternoon a further report from the coastguard said that the *Samba* was still drifting and was now some seventy miles south-east of Lerwick. Two trawlers were now standing by but neither of them had been able to take the *Samba* in tow. A Dutch tug, the *Nord Holland* was on the way. The wind had increased but the master of the *Samba* had said that there was no immediate danger.

At eleven o'clock next morning, the coastguard reported the *Samba* as being now only 19 miles from Bard head, which is at the southern entrance to the approach to Lerwick harbour, and that the Dutch tug had been unable to take her in tow. The casualty had now drifted something like 100 miles in less that 48 hours and was clearly being forced remorselessly towards the rocky cliffs of Shetland and her doom. Not surprisingly, shortly afterwards the master asked for lifeboat assistance and at 1150 the Lerwick lifeboat *Lady Jane and Martha Ryland* left the harbour. The gale continued unabated with a very rough sea and poor visibility.

Soon after noon the Lerwick coxswain, John Sales, received a message by radio telephone from the coastguard informing him that the tug had given her position as 13 miles south by east of Bard head. He altered course for this position but later discovered that the information was wrong. As a result he was too far to the westward of *Samba*, so that he passed her without making contact and proceeded to the southward.

Coxswain Sales soon realised that something was wrong and asked for the latest position of the casualty which was now given as two miles east of Bard head. The wind was now gusting up to 50 knots and it was clear that the *Samba* would be ashore in a matter of minutes if she really was where they said she was. It seemed doubtful whether the lifeboat could possibly reach her in time to effect a rescue.

The skipper of the tug *Nord Holland* realised that the ship must inevitably go ashore and decided to try and take off the crew. Shortly after three o'clock that afternoon he succeeded in rescuing six men by floating a rubber dinghy down to them but the line parted at the second attempt and the dinghy was lost.

Meanwhile the lifeboat was making for the correct position with all speed with a high following sea. One wave broke clean over the stern of the lifeboat and Sales was forced to ease down but he increased speed again on a light being reported off the coast. In addition to the lifeboat a steamer, the *St Clair* and a motor fishing boat, *Harvest Hope* had both put to sea from Lerwick to try and assist in the rescue.

The situation was dramatic in the extreme. The disabled ship had drifted half way across the North sea and a distance of nearly 200 miles since her engines had failed. She was now being driven steadily towards the grim cliffs and rocks of Shetland's rugged coastline. Due to an error in the position she had been given the lifeboat had overshot and steamed away to the south, passing the *Samba* in the poor visibility. In the minds of all who could have known the facts the question must have been 'Can she get back in time to save the lives of those on board?' There was now no question of saving the ship and to add to the difficulties, darkness was falling.

Shortly after five o'clock Coxswain Sales sighted the lights of the tug *Nord Holland* to the north-west of Bard head. Close inshore another faint light could be seen and this he rightly assumed to be from the casualty. In the beam of the lifeboat's searchlight the *Samba* showed up starkly with her bow close under the cliff as she drifted rapidly to the north-west. She must have passed perilously close to Bard head and was now actually in the mouth of Bressay sound, which leads to Lerwick, with cliffs and rocks all round to leeward. There was no escape now.

For the rescue it was now or never. Coxswain Sales did not hesitate but steered across the square stern of *Samba*, almost making contact. As he did so, one of the *Samba*'s crew saw his chance and jumped, landing safely on the deck of the lifeboat and into the waiting arms of her crew.

Over went the wheel as Sales brought the lifeboat round for a second attempt; but this time the high, confused sea frustrated his efforts and there was no chance for a survivor to jump. The seas were breaking right over the casualty whose propellers broke surface as her stern rose high on a wave. The master of the *St Clair* offered to pump oil to reduce the broken water but the coxswain had no time to reply.

Once more the lifeboat turned and made the hair-raising run down wind to close the stern of the *Samba*. To judge the run of the sea and the movement of the casualty with sufficient nicety to ensure contact without disaster needed all the skill and experience of a lifetime of boat-handling. This time two more men leapt to safety.

The fourth attempt proved abortive but the fifth yielded one more survivor in safety while at the sixth run in only the master of the *Samba* remained aboard. He was already exhausted from the strain of the previous days and his jump was nearly fatal as he fell across the fore stay of the lifeboat and would have rolled over the side had it not been for the quick reaction of two lifeboatmen who seized him just in time.

With all the survivors on board the lifeboat set course for her station at Lerwick. Twenty minutes later the *Samba* had driven right across the sound and struck the rocks on the west side. Within 15 minutes the unfortunate vessel had broken up and disappeared.

For this gallant and most efficient service Coxswain John Sales was awarded the bronze medal of the RNLI. It will be agreed that the medal standard in Shetland is very high indeed. The Swedish Lifeboat Society awarded a plaque to the Lerwick station to commemorate the service.

The harbour at Lerwick is frequently used by fishing vessels of other nations and during the season a Norwegian rescue vessel uses it as a base. Russian ships are also regular visitors and some have had reason to be thankful for the efficiency of the Shetland lifeboat service.

On 16 October 1958 the Soviet trawler *Urbe*, believed to have a crew of 35, sank near the Holm of Skaw, an uninhabited rocky islet off the north-eastern corner of the Shetland island of Unst. She was one of a fleet of about 30 vessels fishing off the Shetland isles.

The distress message was transmitted by the Soviet parent

ship *Tomsk* and received by Wick radio. It was passed to the coastguard who in turn informed Mr Bruce Laurenson, honorary secretary of the Lerwick lifeboat station, at nine o'clock that evening.

The Lerwick lifeboat proceeded half an hour later. It was a very dark night with a fresh northerly gale and frequent rain squalls. The Holm of Skaw is some 53 miles north of Lerwick and it was certain that the journey into the teeth of the gale and very rough sea was going to be a testing one for the new lifeboat *Claude Cecil Staniforth*, a 52ft Barnett type.

On their way north a message was received that some survivors had been seen on the Holm of Skaw and at three o'clock on the morning of 17 October Coxswain John Sales called at Baltasound and embarked a Mr Duncan Mouat, who had volunteered to act as pilot. Not long afterwards the starboard propeller of the lifeboat was fouled by a net but Sales closed the southern shore of the Holm on one engine and anchored in ten fathoms of water about 40 yards from the beach.

The wind was gusting a point or two either side of north with a confused sea and heavy swell. There were frequent rain showers and the ebb tide was setting towards the north. Ashore on the island of Unst people had been trying to locate the suvivors. The Baltasound coast rescue team had turned out and had been joined by airmen from the RAF station at Saxa Vord. A Shackleton aircraft and three trawlers had been searching in the vicinity.

In the beam of searchlights the lifeboat's crew could see three survivors from the Soviet ship sheltering behind a large boulder and a rocket was fired, carrying a line across to them. As there was no suitable place on the Holm where the shore end of the line could be made fast, one of the survivors tended the bight by hand while the other two were hauled off to the lifeboat. The third man was the skipper of the Russian trawler and he was hauled off in the breeches buoy, assisting by kicking out vigorously with his legs. While this was going on, other members of the lifeboat's crew managed to clear the fouled propeller.

Coxswain Sales then made for Norwick bay, some two miles away where a small boat was picked up. This was used to make a landing on the Holm where a further search yielded no more survivors and eventually the lifeboat left for

Baltasound. Throughout the rescue and search the parent ship *Tomsk* made repeated requests for the survivors to be returned to her but Coxswain Sales was instructed not to transfer the men at sea in case the lifeboat was damaged in doing so. The survivors received first aid treatment on the lifeboat, being rubbed down, wrapped in blankets and given stimulants. Two dead bodies which had been picked up were also aboard the lifeboat which reached Baltasound at 1245. Here hot baths, meals and refreshments had been prepared by Mrs Charlotte Mouat, owner of the Springfield hotel, who refused any payment and said it was her contribution to the lifeboat service.

Later, after the lifeboat had left Baltasound for Lerwick the coxswain received instructions to return there and land the survivors and the bodies which were subsequently transferred to a Soviet launch.

Among the tributes paid to the work of the Lerwick lifeboat crew was one broadcast by Moscow radio which referred to their 'Brilliant skill, vast courage and selfless heroism'. For this service Coxswain John Sales was awarded the silver medal of the RNLI and Mr Andrew Duncan Mouat of Baltasound was awarded the bronze medal.

Chapter 3
The wreck of the *Indian Chief*

In January 1881 two inspired accounts of the loss of the ship *Indian Chief* appeared in the *Daily Telegraph.* The first gave the story in the words of the mate of the vessel, William Meldrum Lloyd, from the point of view of a survivor and the second described the experiences of the rescuers as related by the coxswain of the lifeboat, Charles Fish. If these were verbatim accounts in the words of the men named it was a brilliant piece of reporting which can rarely if ever have been equalled. Since most seamen have an exceptional facility for describing events connected with the sea it seems probable that the stories of the mate and coxswain were told in the vivid words attributed to them and that some unknown reporter captured a unique piece of sea history.

It happens that at the time in question the *Daily Telegraph* had a contributor or special correspondent in Ramsgate named W. Clark Russell. He was and is well known as a very competent writer of sea stories who had spent some years in sail. Apparently it was either by him or through him that the accounts were written and appeared in the newspaper. However it came about it was a most fortunate circumstance. Not only do these narratives make compelling reading but they also describe a rescue in which a steam tug was used. This towed the lifeboat the 30-odd miles to Long Sand head, right into the wind's eye, a trip that would have been virtually impossible under sail in the prevailing conditions. Although the use of tugs for this purpose was comparatively common at one time there are very few accounts giving details and certainly none to compare with this. For this reason the reports are given here in exactly the same words as when they appeared originally and commence with a description of the scene at Ramsgate harbour when the tug and lifeboat returned with the 11 survivors. It may well have been written by W. Clark Russell himself.

On the afternoon of Thursday the 6th Jan. I made one of a great crowd assembled on the Ramsgate east pier to witness the arrival of the survivors of the crew of a large ship which had gone ashore on the Long Sand early on the preceding Wednesday morning. A heavy gale had been blowing for two days from the north and east; it had moderated somewhat at noon but still stormed fiercely over the surging waters, though a brilliant blue sky arched overhead and a sun shone that made the sea a dazzling surface of broken silver all the way in the south and west. Plunging bows under as she came along, the steamer towed the lifeboat through a haze of spray; but amid this veil of foam, the flags of the two vessels denoting that shipwrecked men were in the boat streamed like well-understood words from the mastheads. The people crowded thickly about the landing steps when the lifeboat entered the harbour. Whispers flew from mouth to mouth. Some said the rescued men were Frenchmen, others that they were Danes, but all were agreed that there was a dead body among them. One by one the survivors came along the pier, the most dismal procession it was ever my lot to behold – eleven live but scarcely living men, most of them clad in oilskins and walking with bowed back, drooping heads and nerveless arms. There was blood on the faces of some, circled with a white encrustation of salt and this same salt filled the hollows of their eyes and streaked their hair with lines that looked like snow.

The first man, who was the chief mate, walked heavily leaning on the arm of the kindly-hearted harbourmaster, Captain Braine. The second man, whose collar-bone was broken, moved as one might suppose a galvanised corpse would. A third man's wan face wore a forced smile which only seemed to light up the piteous, underlying expression of the features. They were all saturated with brine; they were soaked with seawater to the very marrow of the bones. Shivering, and with a stupefied rolling of the eyes, their teeth clenched, their chilled fingers pressed into the palms of their hands, they passed out of sight.

As the last man came I held my breath; he was alive when taken from the wreck but died in the boat. Four men bore him on their shoulders and a flag flung over his face mercifully concealed what was most shocking of the dreadful sight; but they had removed his boots and socks to chafe his feet before he died and had slipped a pair of mittens over the toes, which left the ankles naked. This was the body of Howard Primrose Fraser, the second mate of the ship and her drowned captain's brother. I have often met men newly saved from shipwreck but never remember having beheld more mental anguish and physical suffering than was expressed in the countenances and movements of these eleven sailors. Their story as told to me is a striking and memorable illustration of endurance and hardship on the one hand and of the finest heroical humanity on the other, in every sense worthy to be known to the British public. I got the whole narrative direct from the chief mate, Mr William Meldrum Lloyd, and it shall be related here as nearly as possible in the same words.

The Mate's Account: Our ship was the *Indian Chief*, of 1,238 tons register; our skipper's name was Fraser and we were bound with a general cargo to Yokohama. There were twenty-nine souls on board, counting the north-country pilot. We were four days out from Middlesbrough but it had been thick weather ever since the afternoon of the Sunday on which we sailed. All had gone well with us however, so far, and at half-past two on Wednesday morning we made the Knock light. You must know, sir, that hereabouts the water is just a network of shoals; for to the southward lies the Knock and close over against it stretches the Long sand and beyond, down to the westward, is the Sunk sand.

Shortly after the Knock light hove in sight the wind shifted to the eastward and brought a squall of rain. We were under all plain sail at the time with the exception of the royals, which were furled, and the mainsail that hung in the buntlines. The Long sand was to leeward and finding that we were drifting that way the order was given to put the ship about. It was very dark, the wind breezing up sharper and sharper and as cold as death. The helm was put down but the main braces fouled and before they could be cleared the vessel missed stays and was in irons. We went to work to wear the ship but there was much confusion, the vessel heeling over and all of us knew that the sands were close abroad. The ship paid off but at a critical moment the spanker boom sheet fouled the wheel. Still, we managed to get the vessel round but scarcely were the braces belayed and the ship on the starboard tack when she struck the ground broadside on.

She was a soft-wood built ship and she trembled as though she would go to pieces at once like a pack of cards. Sheets and halliards were let go but no man durst venture aloft. Every moment threatened to bring the spars crashing about us and the thundering and beating of the canvas made the masts buckle and jump like fishing-rods. We then kindled a great flare and sent up rockets and our signals were answered by the Sunk lightship and the Knock. We could see one another's faces in the light of the big blaze and sung out cheerily to keep our hearts up; and indeed, sir, although we all knew that our ship was hard and fast and likely to leave her bones on that sand we none of us reckoned upon dying. The sky had cleared, the easterly wind made the stars sharp and bright and it was comforting to watch the lightships' rockets rushing up and bursting into smoke and sparks over our heads. For they made us see that our position was known and they were as good as an assurance that help would come along soon and that we need not lose heart. But all this time the wind was gradually sweeping up into a gale – and oh, the cold, good Lord, the bitter cold of that wind!

It seemed as long as a month before the morning broke and just before the grey grew broad in the sky one of the men yelled out something and then came sprawling and splashing aft to tell us that he had caught sight of the sail of a lifeboat, dodging among the heavy seas.* We rushed to the side to look, half blinded by the spray and the wind and clutching at whatever offered to our hands. When at last we caught sight of the lifeboat we cheered and the leaping of my heart made me feel sick and death-like. As the dawn brightened we could see more plainly and it was frightful to notice how the men looked at her, meeting the stinging spray borne on the wind without a wink of the eye that they might not lose sight of the boat for an instant, the salt whitening their faces all the while like a layer of flour as they watched.

She was a good distance away and she stood on and off, never coming closer and obviously shirking the huge seas

* This was an error as no lifeboat could possibly have been near the wreck at that early hour as news was not received until eleven o'clock that day. It was probably the smack which conveyed the news of the wreck to Harwich, where she arrived at eleven in the morning.

which were now boiling around us. At last she hauled her sheet aft, put her helm over and went away. One of our crew groaned but no other man uttered a sound and we returned to the shelter of the deckhouse.

Though the gale was not at its height when the sun rose it was not far from it. We plucked up spirits when the sun shot out of a raging sea but as we lay broadside on to the waves the sheets of flying water soon made the sloping decks a dangerous place for a man to stand on. The crew and officers kept to the shelter of the deckhouses, though the captain, his brother and I were constantly going out to see if any help was coming. But now the flood was making and this was a fresh and fearful danger, as we all knew. At sunrise the water had been too low to knock the ship out of her sandy bed but as the tide rose it lifted the vessel, bumping her and straining her frightfully. The pilot advised the skipper to let go the starboard anchor, hoping that the tide would slew the ship's stern round and make her lie head to seas. So the anchor was dropped but it did not alter the ship's position. To know, sir, what the cracking and straining of that vessel was like, as bit by bit she slowly went to pieces, you must have been aboard of her. When she broke her back a sort of panic seized many of us and the captain roared out to the men to get the boats over and see if any use could be made of them. Three boats were launched but the second boat, with two hands in her, went adrift and was instantly engulfed, the poor fellows in her vanishing as you might blow out a light. The other boats filled as soon as they touched the water. There was no help for us that way and again we withdrew to the cabins. A little before five o'clock in the afternoon a huge sea swept the vessel, clearing the decks fore and aft and leaving little standing but the uprights of the deckhouses. It was a dreadful sea but we knew that worse was behind it and that we must climb the rigging if we wanted to prolong our lives. The hold was already full of water and portions of the deck had been blown out, so that everywhere great yawning gulfs met the eye, with the black water washing almost flush. Some of the men made for the fore-rigging but the captain shouted to all hands to take to the mizenmast as that one, in his opinion, was the most secure. A number of the men who were scrambling forward returned on hearing the captain sing out but the rest held on and gained the foretop.

Seventeen of us got over the mizentop and with our knives fell to hacking away at such running gear as we could come at, to serve as lashings. None of us touched the mainmast for we all knew, now that the ship had broken her back, that that spar was doomed. The reason why the captain had called to the men to come aft was because he was afraid that when the mainmast went it would drag the foremast, that rocked the ship with every movement, with it.

I was next the captain in the mizentop and near him was his brother, a stout-built, handsome young fellow, twenty-two years old, as fine a specimen of the English sailor as ever I was shipmates with. He was calling about him cheerfully, bidding us not to be down-hearted and telling us to look sharply round for the lifeboats. He helped several of the benumbed men to lash themselves, saying encouraging things to them as he made them fast. As the sun sank the wind became more freezing and I saw the strength of some of the men lashed over me leaving them fast. The captain shook hands with me and, on the chance of my being saved, gave me some messages to take home, too sacred to be written down, sir. He likewise handed me his watch and chain and I put them in my pocket. The canvas streamed in ribbons from the yards and the noise was like a continuous roll of thunder overhead. It was dreadful to look down and see the decks ripping up and notice that every sea that rolled over the wreck left less of her than it found.

The moon went quickly away – it was a young moon with little power – but the white water and the starlight kept the night from being black. The frame of the vessel stood out like a sketch done in ink every time the dark seas ran clear of her and left her visible upon the foam. There was no talking, no calling to one another, the men hung in the topmast rigging like corpses. I noticed the second mate to windward of his brother in the top, sheltering him as best he could, poor fellow, from the wind that went through our skins like a shower of arrows.

On a sudden I took it into my head to fancy that the mizenmast was not so secure as the foremast. It came into my mind like a fright and I called to the captain that I meant to make for the foretop. I don't know whether he heard me or whether he made any answer. Maybe it was a sort of craze of mine for the moment, for I was wild with eagerness to leave that mast as soon as ever I began to fear for it. I cast my lashings adrift and gave a look at the deck and saw that I must not go that way if I did not want to be drowned. So I climbed into the crosstrees and swung myself on to the stay, so reaching the maintop. Then I scrambled on to the main topmast crosstrees and went hand over hand down the topmast stay into the foretop. Had I reflected before I left the mizentop I should not have believed that I had the strength to work my way forward like that. My hands felt as if they were skinned and my finger joints appeared to have no use in them. There were nine or ten men in the foretop, all lashed and huddled together. The mast rocked sharply and the throbbing of it to the blowing of the great tatters of canvas was a horrible sensation. From time to time they sent up rockets from the Sunk lightship – once every hour, I should think – but we had long since ceased to notice those signals. There was not a man but thought his time had come and, though death seemed terrible as I looked down upon the boiling waters below, yet the anguish of the cold almost killed the craving for life.

It was now about three o'clock on the Thursday morning; the air was full of the strange, dim light of the foam and the stars and I could very plainly see the black swarm of men in the top and rigging of the mizenmast. I was looking that way when a great sea fell upon the hull of the ship with a fearful crash; a moment after the mainmast went. It fell quickly, and as it fell it bore down the mizenmast. There was a horrible noise of splintering wood and some piercing cries and then another great sea swept over the after deck and we who were in the foretop looked and saw the stumps of the two masts sticking up from the bottom of the hold, the mizenmast slanting over the bulwarks into the water and the men lashed to it drowning.

There was never a more shocking sight and the wonder is that some of us that saw it did not go raving mad. The foremast still stood, complete to the royal mast and all the yards across but every instant I expected to find myself hurtling through the air. By this time the ship was completely gutted, the upper part of her a mere frame of ribs, and the gale still blew furiously; indeed, I gave up hope when the mizenmast fell and I saw my shipmates drowning on it.

It was half an hour after this that a man, who was jammed close against me, pointed out into the darkness and cried in a wild, hoarse voice 'Isn't that a steamer's light?' I looked, but what with grief and suffering and cold I was nearly blinded and could see nothing. But presently another man called out that he could see a light and this was echoed by yet another, so I told them to keep their eyes on it and watch if it moved. They said by-and-by that it was stationary and though we could not guess that it meant anything good for us, yet this light heaving in sight and our talking of it gave us some comfort.

When dawn broke we saw the smoke of a steamer and agreed that it was her light that we had seen; but I made nothing of the smoke and was looking heart-brokenly at the mizenmast and the cluster of drowned men washing about it when a loud cry made me turn my head and then I saw a life-boat under reefed foresail heading direct for us. It was a sight, sir, to make one crazy with joy and it put the strength of ten men into every one of us. A man named Gillmore – I think it was Gillmore – stood up and waved a long strip of canvas. But I believe they had seen that there were living men aboard before the signal was made. The boat had to cross the broken water to fetch us and in my agony of mind I cried out 'She'll never face it! She'll leave us when she sees that water!' for the sea was frightful all to windward of the sand and over it – a tremendous play of broken waters, raging one with another and making the whole surface a boiling cauldron. Yet they never swerved a hair's breadth. Oh, sir, she was a noble boat! We could see her crew – twelve of them – sitting on the thwarts, all looking our way, motionless as carved figures, and there was not a stir among them as, in an instant, the boat leapt from the crest of a towering sea right into the monstrous broken tumble. The peril of those men, who were risking their lives to save ours, made us forget our own situation. Over and over again the boat was buried but as regularly did she emerge with her crew looking fixedly our way and their oilskins and the light-coloured side of the boat sparkling in the sunshine, while the coxswain, leaning forward from the tiller, watched our ship with a face of iron.

By this time we knew that this boat was here to save us and that she *would* save us and with wildly beating hearts we unlashed ourselves and dropped over the top into the rigging. We were all sailors you see, sir, and knew what the lifeboatmen wanted and what was to be done. Swift as thought we bent a number of ropes' ends together and securing a bit of wood to this line, threw it overboard and let it drift to the boat. It was seized and a hawser made fast and we dragged the great rope on board. By means of this rope the lifeboatmen hauled their craft under our quarter, clear of the raffle. But there was no such rush made for her as might be thought. No, I owe it to my shipmates to say this. Two of them shinned out upon the mizenmast to the body of the second mate, that was lashed eight or nine feet away over the side, and got him into the boat before they entered it themselves. I heard the coxswain of the boat – Charles Fish by name, this fittest man in the world for that berth and this work – cry out 'Take that poor fellow in there!' and he pointed to the body of the captain, which was lashed in the top with arms over the mast, head erect and eyes wide open. But one of our crew called out 'He's been dead four hours, sir,' and then the rest of us scrambled into the boat, looking away from the dreadful group of drowned men that lay in a cluster round the fallen mast. The second mate was alive but a maniac; it was heartbreaking to hear his broken, feeble cries for his brother. He lay quiet after a bit and died in half an hour, though we chafed his feet and poured rum into his mouth, doing what men in our miserable plight could do for a fellow sufferer.

Nor were we out of danger yet, for the broken water was enough to turn a man's hair grey to look at. It was a fearful sea for us men to find ourselves in the midst of, after having looked at it from a great height and I felt at the beginning that I should have been safer on the wreck than in the lifeboat. Never could I have believed that so small a vessel could meet such a sea and live. Yet she rose like a duck to the great roaring waves which followed her, draining every drop of water from the bottom of the boat as she was hove up and falling with terrible suddenness into a hollow, only to bound like a living thing to the summit of the next gigantic crest.

When I looked at the lifeboat's crew and thought of our situation a short while since, and how to rescue us these great-hearted men had imperilled their own lives, I was unmanned; I could not thank them, I could not trust myself to speak. They told us they had left Ramsgate harbour early on the preceding afternoon and had fetched the Knock at dusk. Not seeing our wreck had lain to in that raging sea, suffering almost as severely as ourselves, all through the piercing tempestuous night. What do you think of such a service, sir? How can such devoted heroism be written of, so that every man who can read shall know how great and beautiful it is? Our own suffering came to us as part of our calling as seamen. But theirs was bravely courted and endured for the sake of their fellow creatures. Believe me, sir, it was a splendid piece of service, nothing grander in its way was ever done before, even by Englishmen. I am a plain seaman and can say no more about it all than this. But when I think what must have come to us eleven men before another hour had passed if the lifeboat crew had not run down to us, I feel like a little child and my heart grows too full for my eyes.

Two days had elapsed, continued the writer in the *Daily Telegraph*, since the rescue of the survivors of the crew of the *Indian Chief* and I was gazing with much interest at the victorious lifeboat as she lay motionless on the water of the harbour. It was a very calm day, the sea stretching from the pier sides as smooth as a piece of green silk and growing vague in the wintry haze of the horizon, while the white cliffs were brilliant with the winter sunshine. It filled the mind with strange and moving thoughts to look at that lifeboat, with her image as sharp as a coloured photograph shining in the clear water under her, and then reflect upon the furious conflict she had been concerned in only two nights before; the freight of half drowned men that had loaded her, the dead body on her thwart, the bitter cold of the howling gale, the deadly peril that had attended every heave of the huge black seas. Within a few hundred yards of her lay the tug, the sturdy steamer that had towed her to the Long sand, that had held her astern all night and brought her back safe on the following afternoon.

The tug had suffered much from the frightful tossing she had received and her injuries had not yet been dealt with. She had lost her sponsons, her starboard side-house had gone, the port side of her bridge had been started and the iron railings warped, her decks still seemed dank from the continuous washing, her funnel was brown with rust and the tough craft looked a hundred years old. Remembering what these vessels had gone through, how they had but two days since topped a long series of merciful and dangerous errands by as brilliant an act of heroism and humanity as any on record, it was difficult to behold them without a quickened pulse.

I recalled the coming ashore of their crews; the lifeboatmen with their great cork jackets around them, the steamer's men in streaming oilskins, the faces of many of them livid with cold, their eyes dim with the bitter vigil they had kept and the furious blowing of the spray. I remembered the bright smile that here and there lighted up the weary faces as first one and then another caught sight of a wife or a sister in the crowd waiting to greet and accompany the brave hearts to the warmth of their humble homes. I felt that while these crews' sufferings and the courage and resolution they had shown remained unwritten, only half of a very stirring story had been recorded. The narrative, as related to me by the coxswain of the lifeboat is a necessary pendant to the tale told last week by the mate of the wrecked ship and as the coxswain and his colleagues, both of the lifeboat and the steam tug need no better introduction than their own deeds, let Charles Edward Fish begin his yarn without further preface.

The Coxswain's Account: News had been brought to Ramsgate as you know, sir, that a large ship was ashore on the Long sand and Captain Braine, the harbour-master, immediately ordered the tug and the lifeboat to proceed to her assistance. It was blowing a heavy gale of wind although it was blowing much harder some hours afterwards. The moment we were clear of the piers we felt the sea. Our boat is a very fine one. I know there is no better on the coasts and there are only two in Great Britain bigger. She was presented to the Lifeboat Institution by Bradford and is called after that town. But it is ridiculous to talk of bigness when it means only forty-two feet long and when the sea is raging round you heavy enough to swamp a line-of-battle ship. I had my eye on the tug – named the *Vulcan*, sir, – when she met the first of the seas and she was thrown up like a ball. You could see her starboard paddle revolving in the air high enough for a coach to pass under and when she struck the hollow she dished a sea over her bows that left only the stern of her showing. We were towing head to wind and the water was flying over the boat in clouds. Every man of us was soaked to the skin in spite of our overalls by the time we had brought the Ramsgate sands abeam. But there were a good many miles to be gone over before we should fetch the Knock lightship and so you see, sir, it was much too early for us to take notice that things were not over and above comfortable.

We got out the sail-cover – a piece of tarpaulin – to make a shelter of and rigged it up against the mast, seizing it to the burtons, but it had not been up two minutes when a heavy sea washed it right aft in rags. So there was nothing to do but hold on to the thwarts and shake ourselves when the sea came over. I never remember a colder wind. I don't say this because I happened to be out in it. Old Tom Cooper, one of the best boatmen in all England, who made one of our crew, agreed with me that it was more like a flaying machine than a natural gale of wind. The feel of it was like being gnawed in the face by a dog; I only wonder it didn't freeze the tears it fetched out of our eyes. We were heading north-east and the wind was blowing from the north-east. The North Foreland had been a bit of shelter, like, but when we got clear of that and the ocean lay ahead of us the sea were furious. They seemed miles long, like an Atlantic sea and it was enough to make a man hold his breath to watch how the tug wallowed and tumbled into them. I sung out to Dick Goldsmith, 'Dick,' I says, 'She's slowed, do you see, she'll never be able to meet it,' for she had slackened her engines down to a mere crawl and I really did think that they meant to give up. I could see Alf Page – the master of her, sir, – coming and going like the moon when the clouds sweep over it, as the seas smothered him up one minute and left him shining in the sun the next. But there was no giving up with the tug's crew any more than there was with the lifeboat's; she held on and we followed.

Somewhere about the Elbow buoy a smack that was running ported her helm to speak to us. Her skipper just had time to yell out 'A vessel on the Long sand!' and we to wave our hands when she was astern and out of sight in a haze of spray. Presently a collier named the *Fanny*, with her foretopgallant yard gone passed us. She was cracking on to bring the news of the wreck to Ramsgate and was making a heavy splutter under her topsails and foresail. They raised a cheer for they knew our errand and then, like the smack she was astern and gone. By this time the cold and the wet and the fearful plunging were beginning to tell and one of the men called for a nip of rum. The quantity we generally take is half a gallon and it is always my rule to be sparing with that drink for the sake of the shipwrecked men we may have to bring home and who are pretty sure to be in greater need of the stuff than us. I never drink myself, sir, and that's one reason, I think, why I manage to meet the cold and wet middling well and rather better than some men who look stronger than me. However I told Charlie Verrion to measure the rum out and serve it round. It would have made you laugh, I do believe, sir, to have seen the care the men took with that big bottle – Charlie cocking his finger into the cork hole and Davy Berry clapping his hand over the pewter measure whenever a sea came to prevent the salt water from spoiling the liquor. Bad as our plight was, the tug's crew were no better off. Their wheel is forrard and so you may suppose that the fellow who steered had his share of the seas. The others stood by to relieve him and, for the matter of water she was just like a rock, the waves striking her bows and flying pretty nigh as high as the top of her funnel and blowing the whole length of her aft with a fall like the tumble of half a dozen cartloads of bricks. I like to speak of what they went through for the way they were knocked about was something fearful, to be sure.

By half-past four o'clock in the afternoon it was drawing on dusk and about that hour we sighted the revolving light of the Kentish Knock lightship and a little after five we were pretty close to her. She is a big, red hulled boat, with the words Kentish Knock written in long white letters on her sides. Dark as it was we could see her flung up and rushing down fit to roll her over and over. The way she pitched and went out of sight and then ran up on the black heights of water gave me a better notion of the fearfulness of that sea than I had got by watching the tug or noticing our own lively dancing.

The tug hailed her first and two men looking over her side answered but what they said didn't reach the lifeboat. Then the steamer towed us abreast but the tide caught our warp and gave us a sheer that brought us much too close alongside her. When the sea took her she seemed to hang right over us and the sight of that great dark hull, looking as if when it fell it must come right on top of us, made us want to sheer off, I can tell you.

I sung out 'Have you seen the ship?' and one of the men bawled back 'Yes.'

'How does she bear?'

'Nor'-west by north.'

'Have you seen anything go to her?'

The answer I caught was 'A boat.'

Some of our men said the answer was a 'lifeboat' but most of us heard only 'a boat'.

The tug was now towing ahead and we went past the lightship but ten minutes after Tom Friend sings out 'They're burning a light aboard her,' and looking astern I saw they had fired a red signal light that was blazing over the bulwark in a long shower of sparks.

The tug put her helm down to return and we were brought broadside to the sea. Then we felt the power of those waves, sir. It looked a wonder that we were not rolled over and drowned, every one of us. We held on with our teeth clenched and twice the boat was filled and the water up to our throats. 'Look out for it, men' was always the cry. But every upward scend emptied the noble little craft, like pulling out a plug in a washbasin and in a few minutes we were again alongside the lightvessel. This time there were six or seven men looking over the side.

'What do you want?' we shouted.

'Did you see the Sunk lightship's rocket?' they all yelled together.

'Yes, did you say you saw a boat?'

'No,' they answered, showing that we had mistaken their first reply. On which I shouted to the tug 'Pull us round to the Long sand head buoy,' and then we were under way again, meeting the tremendous seas.

There was only a little bit of moon, westering fast and what there was of it showed only now and again as the heavy clouds opened up and let the light of it down. Indeed, it was very dark, though there was some kind of glimmer in the foam which allowed us to mark the tug ahead.

'Bitter cold work, Charlie,' says old Tom Cooper to me, 'But,' he says, 'It's colder for the poor wretches aboard the wreck, if they're alive to feel it.'

The thought of them made our own sufferings small and we kept looking and looking into the darkness around but there was nothing to be spied, only now and again, and a long whiles apart, the flash of a rocket in the sky from the Sunk lightship.

Meanwhile from time to time we burnt a hand signal – a light that's fired something after the manner of a gun. You fit it into a wooden tube and give a sort of hammer at the end a smart blow and the flame rushes out and a bright light it makes, sir. Ours were green lights and whenever I set one flaring I couldn't help noticing the appearance of the men. It was a queer sight I assure you, to see them all as green as leaves with their cork jackets swelling out their bodies so as to scarcely seem like human beings and the black water as high as our masthead or howling a long way below us on either side.

They burned hand-signals on the tug, too, but nothing came of them. There was no sign of the wreck and staring over the edge of the boat, with the spray and the darkness was like trying to see through the bottom of a well. So we began to talk the matter over and Tom Cooper says, 'We had better stop here and wait for daylight.'

'I'm for stopping,' says Steve Goldsmith and Bob Penny says 'We're here to fetch the wreck and fetch it we will, if we wait a week.'

'Right,' says I; and all hands being agreed – without any fuss although I dare say most of our hearts were at home and our wishes alongside our hearths and the warm fires in them – we all of us put our hands to our mouths and made one great cry of '*Vulcan* ahoy'. The tug dropped astern.

'What do you want?' sings out the skipper when he gets within speaking distance.

'There's nothing to be seen of the vessel and so we had better lie-to for the night,' I answered.

'Very good,' says he and then the steamer, without another word from her crew, with the water tumbling over her bows like cliffs, resumed her station ahead, her paddles just revolving fast enough to keep her from dropping astern.

As the coxswain of the lifeboat I take no credit for resolving to lie-to all night. But I am bound to say a word for the two crews, who made up their minds without a murmur, without a second's hesitation, to face the bitter cold and fierce seas of that long winter darkness that they might be on the spot to help their fellow creatures when dawn broke and showed them where they were.

I know that there are scores of sailors round our coasts who would have done likewise. Only read, sir, what was done in the north, Newcastle way, during the gales last October. But surely, no matter who may be the men who do what they think their duty, whether they belong to the north or the south, they deserve encouragement and praise. A man likes to feel, when he has done his best, that his fellow-men think well of his work. If I had not been one of the crew I would wish to say more; but no false pride shall make me say less, sir, and I thank God for the resolution he put into us, and for the strength He gave us to keep that resolution.

All we had to do now was to make ourselves as comfortable as we could. Our tow rope veered us out a long way; too far astern for the tug to help us as a breakwater. The manner in which we were flung towards the sky, with half our keel out of the water and then dropped into a hollow – like falling from the top of a house – while the heads of the seas blew into and tumbled over us all the time, made us all reckon that, so far from getting any rest, most of our time would be spent in preventing ourselves from being washed overboard.

We turned to and got the foresail aft and made a kind of roof of it. This was no easy job for the wind was so furious that wrestling even that bit of sail was like fighting with a steam-engine. When it was up ten of us snugged ourselves away under it and two men stood on the after-grating thwart keeping a lookout, with the lifelines around them. As you know, sir, we carry a binnacle and the lamp in it was alight and gave out just enough haze for us to see each other in. We all lay in a lump for warmth and a fine show we made, I dare say; for a cork jacket, even when a man stands upright isn't calculated to improve his figure and as we all of us had cork jackets on with oilskins and many of us sea boots, you may guess what a raffle of arms and legs we showed. What a rum heap of odds and ends we must have looked as we sprawled in the bottom of the boat upon one another.

Sometimes it would be Johnny Goldsmith – for we had three Goldsmiths, Steve, Dick and Johnny – growling underneath that someone was lying on his leg; and then maybe Harry Meader would bawl out that someone was sitting on his head. Once Tom Friend swore his arm was broke but my opinion is that it was too cold to feel inconveniences of this kind. I believe that some among us would not have known if their arms and legs really had been broke, until they tried to use them, for the cold seemed to take away all feeling out of the blood.

As the seas flew over the boat the water filled the sail that was stretched overhead and bellied it down upon us. That gave us less room so that some had to lie flat on their faces;

but when the bellying got too bad we'd all get up and make one heave with our backs under the sail and chuck the water out of it in this way.

'Charlie Fish,' says Tom Cooper to me in a grave voice, 'What would some of them young gen'lemen as comes to Ramsgate in the summer and says they'd like to go out in the lifeboat, think of this?'

This made me laugh and then young Tom Cooper votes for another nipper of rum all round. As it was then drawing on for one o'clock in the morning and some of the men were groaning with cold and pressing themselves against the thwarts with the pain of it I made no objection and the liquor went round.

I always take a cake of Fry's chocolate with me when I go out in the lifeboat as I find it very supporting. I had a mind to have a mouthful now but when I opened the locker I found it full of water, my chocolate nothing but paste and the biscuits a mass of pulp. This was rather hard as there was nothing else to eat and there was no getting near the tug in that sea unless we wished to be smashed into staves. However, we didn't come out to enjoy ourselves; nothing was said and so we lay in a heap, hugging one another for warmth, until morning broke.

The first man to look to leeward was old Tom's son – young Tom Cooper – and in a moment he bawled out, 'There she is,' pointing like a madman.

The morning had only just broke and the light was grey and dim. Down in the west it still seemed to be night. The air was full of spray and scarcely were we atop of a sea than we were rushing like an arrow into the hollow again, so that young Tom must have had eyes like a hawk to have seen her. Yet the moment he sung out and pointed all hands cried out, 'There she is.'

But what was it, sir? Only a mast about three miles off – just one single mast sticking up out of the white water, as thin and faint as a spider's line. Yet that was the ship we had been waiting all night to see. There she was and my heart thumped in my ears the moment my eye fell on that mast.

But Lord, sir, the fearful sea that was raging between her and us! For where we were was in deepish water and the waves regular; but all about the wreck was the sand and the water on it was running in a fury in all sorts of ways – rushing up in a tall column of foam as high as a ship's main-yard and thundering so loudly that, though we were to windward, we could hear it above the gale and the boiling of the seas round us. It might have shook even a man who wanted to die to look at it if he didn't know what the *Bradford* can go through. I ran my eye over the men's faces.

'Let slip the tow rope,' bawled Dick Goldsmith.

'Up foresail,' I shouted and in two minutes from the time we had sighted the mast we were dead before the wind, our storm foresail taut as a drumskin, our boat's stem heading full for the broken seas and the lonely, stranded vessel in the midst of them. It was as well that there was something in front of us to keep our eyes that way and that none of us thought of looking astern or the sight of the high and frightful seas that raged after us might have played old Harry with weak nerves. Some of them came with such force that they leapt right over the boat and the air was dark with water flying a dozen yards high over us in solid sheets, which fell with a roar like the explosion of a gun, ten or a dozen fathoms ahead. But we took no notice of these seas even when we were in the thick of the broken water, with all hands holding on to the thwarts for dear life. Every thought was on the mast which was growing bigger and clearer and sometimes when the sea hove us high we could just see the hull, with the water as white as milk flying over it. The mast was what they call 'bright', that is, scraped and varnished and we knew that if there was anything alive aboard that doomed ship we should find it on that mast. We strained our eyes with all our might but could see nothing that looked like a man.

But on a sudden I caught sight of a length of canvas streaming out of the top and all of us seeing it we raised a shout and a few minutes after we saw the men. They were all dressed in yellow oilskins and the mast being that colour was the reason we did not see them sooner. They looked a whole mob of people and one of us roared out 'All hands are there, men,' and I answered 'Aye, the whole ship's company and we'll have them all,' for though as we afterwards knew there was only eleven of them, yet as I have said, they looked a great number huddled together in the top and I made sure the whole ship's company was there.

By this time we were pretty close to the ship and a fearful wreck she looked, with her mainmast and mizenmast gone and her bulwarks washed away and great lumps of timber and planking ripping out of her and going overboard with every pour of the seas. We let go our anchor fifteen fathoms to windward of her and as we did so the poor chaps unlashed themselves and dropped one by one over the top into the lee rigging.

As we veered out our cable and drove down under her stern I shouted to the men on the wreck to bend a piece of wood on to a line and throw it overboard for us to lay hold of. They did this but they had to get aft first and I feared for the half-perished creatures again and again as I saw them scrambling along the lee rail, stopping and holding on as the mountainous seas swept over the hull and then creeping a bit further aft in the lull. There was a horrible muddle of spars and torn canvas and rigging under her lee but we could not guess what a fearful sight was there until our hawser having been made fast to the wreck we hauled the lifeboat close under her quarter.

There looked to be a whole score of dead bodies knocking about among the spars. It stunned me for a moment for I had thought all hands were in the foretop and never dreamt of so many lives being lost. Seventeen were drowned and there they were, most of them, with the body of the captain lashed to the mizzenmast, so as to look as if he were leaning over it, his head stiff upright and his eyes watching us and the stir of the seas made it look as if he were struggling to get to us.

I thought he was alive and cried to the men to hand him in but someone said he was killed when the mizzenmast fell and had been dead four or five hours. This was a dreadful shock; I never remember the like of it. I can't hardly get those fixed eyes out of my sight and I lie awake for hours of a night and so does Tom Cooper and others of us, seeing those bodies turned by the spars and bleeding, floating in the water alongside that miserable ship.

Well, sir, the rest of this lamentable story has been told by the mate of the ship and I don't know that I could add anything to it. We saved the eleven men and I have since heard that they are all doing well. If I may speak, as coxswain of the lifeboat I would like to say that all hands concerned in this rescue, them in the tug as well as the crew of the boat, did what might be expected of English sailors – for such they are, whether you call them boatmen or not; and I know in my heart and say it without fear, that from the time of leaving Ramsgate harbour to the moment when we sighted the wreck's mast, there was only one thought in all of us and that was that the Almighty would give us strength and direct us how to save the lives of the poor fellows to whose assistance we had been sent.

For this service Coxswain Charles Fish was awarded the gold medal of the Institution. Eighteen silver medals were awarded, eleven to the other members of the crew of the Ramsgate lifeboat and seven to the crew of the tug *Vulcan.*

Chapter 4
Gold medal rescues

The gold medal of the RNLI is often known as the lifeboatman's VC and indeed it is normally only bestowed for deeds of exceptional courage and resource. On very rare occasions the gold medal has been awarded to honour some outstanding contribution to the work of the RNLI as when a presentation was made to Princess Marina, Duchess of Kent, to mark the completion of her 25 years as President of the Institution. The founder of the RNLI, Sir William Hillary, was awarded four gold medals, the first in recognition of his work in starting the service but the other three were all earned in taking part in daring rescues.

When it is considered that a particularly fine service has been performed the details are closely investigated on the spot and a recommendation made to the committee of management of the RNLI, if it is felt that a special award should be made. This could take the form of either a gold medal, silver medal, bronze medal or the Thanks of the Institution inscribed on vellum. It is not only at the RNLI headquarters that the standard for medal awards is kept high but the crews on the coast are also jealous of this. Some years ago the coxswain of the Fleetwood lifeboat was awarded a bronze medal which some members of the RNLI committee thought should have been a silver one. When the Fleetwood coxswain was told of the award he was almost indignant and said he really did not think it had been a medal service by Fleetwood standards. It is true that lifeboatmen are a race of plain speaking individualists and know precisely what their job is all about.

Undoubtedly one of the finest rescues by lifeboat and one of extreme hardship and endurance as well as danger was that of the crew of the Daunt rock lightvessel off the south coast of Ireland by the Ballycotton lifeboat.

This great rescue was vividly reported at the time by Robert Mahony, honorary secretary of the Ballycotton lifeboat station, and cannot be told better than in his own words.

'On Friday, 7 February 1936, a gale from the south-east sprang up on the south coast of Ireland with a very heavy sea. The gale increased until, about midnight on the following Monday, it was blowing a hurricane force never experienced before in the memory of the oldest inhabitant of Ballycotton. Huge waves were smashing over the pier and breakwater. The harbour was a seething cauldron. At high water on the Monday evening nothing could be seen of the breakwater or the pier.

'During the Sunday and early Monday the coxswain ran ropes from the lifeboat, the *Mary Stanford*, a 51ft Barnett motor lifeboat, to prevent her from striking the breakwater, as the boat lay afloat. At midnight on the Monday when the gale had risen to a hurricane, the coxswain's own motorboat was seen to have parted her moorings and was in danger of being carried out to sea. The coxswain and several other men attempted to launch a boat to her but were nearly swamped. Stones about a ton in weight were being torn from the quay and being flung about like lumps of sugar. I spent most of the night near the lifeboathouse, watching the terrible destruction that the wind and waves were doing. Twice I was spun round and nearly flung on my face. At three on the Tuesday morning I went to bed but not to sleep. I was out again shortly after seven and found that the coxswain and the other men had been up all night trying to secure his motorboat. They had succeeded in launching a boat, got a rope to the motorboat and secured her. It was at that moment, after this long night of anxiety, that the call for the lifeboat came.

'The men were just back when the Civic Guard at Ballycotton rang me up. A messenger had arrived – for all telephone communication except local lines had broken down twenty-four hours before – with a message that the Daunt rock lightship, with eight men on board, had broken from her moorings twelve miles away and was drifting towards Ballycotton.

'I gave the coxswain the message and he made no reply. I had seen the weather. Seas were breaking over the boathouse, where the boarding boat was kept. I did not believe it possible even for the coxswain to get aboard the lifeboat at her moorings. I was afraid to order him out.

'He left and went down to the harbour. I followed a little later. To my amazement the lifeboat was already at the harbour mouth, dashing out between the piers. The coxswain had not waited for orders. His crew were already at the harbour. He had not fired the maroons for he did not want to alarm the village. Without a word they had slipped away. As I watched the lifeboat I thought every minute she must turn back. At one moment a sea crashed on her; at the next she was standing on her heel. But she went on. People watching her left the quay to go to church to pray. I watched her until she was a mile off, at the lighthouse, where she met seas so mountainous that their spray as we could see – and the lighthouse keeper verified later – was flying over the lantern 196 feet high. At the lighthouse the lifeboat seemed to hesitate. She turned round. We thought she was coming back. Then to our horror the coxswain took her through the sound between the two islands. That way, as we knew, though it was much more dangerous than the open sea, he would save half a mile.

'He took her through the sound after consulting with the second coxswain and there, as I learnt afterwards, the seas were tremendous. The lifeboat came off the top of one sea and dropped into the trough of the next with such a terrible thud that everyone thought that the engines had gone through the bottom of the boat, but the motor mechanic reported, "All's well. After that she will go through anything!" The coxswain now had the whole crew in the after cockpit and after each sea that filled it he counted his men.

'He drove the lifeboat safely through the sound and then had a run before the wind along the coast. When he was off Ballycroneen, about six miles from Ballycotton, the following seas got worse and the coxswain decided to put out the drogue to steady the boat. He eased the engines to do it and several seas struck him on the head, half stunning him. Then as the drogue was being put out a great curling sea came over the port quarter. It filled the cockpit knocking down every man on board. When they recovered they found that the drogue ropes had fouled but the drogue was drawing.

'The lifeboat ran in towards the shore but in the spray, rain and sleet it was not visible; nothing of the lightship could be seen. The coxswain then decided to make for the usual position of the lightship and put the boat's head to sea. He went on for seven miles to what he thought her position had been but owing to the erratic course he had taken and the rain and sleet, he could not be sure. There was still no sign of her and he decided to run to Queenstown for information. (The boat had no wireless at this time.) He reached Queenstown at eleven o'clock that morning after a trying time for he now had no drogue to help him through the breaking seas in the mouth of the harbour and used the oil sprays to calm the breakers a little. At Queenstown he got the exact position of the lightship from the pilots; he tried to telephone me at Ballycotton but found that the wires were still down and put to sea once again.

'Just after midday he found the lightship. She had got an anchor down and was a quarter of a mile south-west of the Daunt rock and half a mile from the shore. HM destroyer *Tenedos* and the SS *Innisfallen* were standing by her. When the lifeboat arrived the *Innisfallen* left.

'The coxswain spoke to the crew of the lightvessel. They did not want to leave her for they knew the danger it was to navigation that the lightship was out of position. But they feared their anchor would not hold and they asked the lifeboat to stand by. This she did. It was too bad to anchor but she kept slowly steaming and drifting.

'About three-thirty, when the gale had eased a little, the *Tenedos* anchored to windward of the lightship, dropped down towards her and tried to float a grass line to her with a buoy attached, in order to get a wire cable to her and take her in tow. This failed. The lifeboat then picked up the buoy and got close enough to the lightship to pass it to her. This time they got the towing line aboard but then the wire parted. These attempts had taken nearly two hours and the *Tenedos*, the lifeboat and the lightship had been continuously swept by heavy seas. It was now dark and impossible to make another attempt to take the lightship in tow. As the *Tenedos* was going to stand by all night the coxswain decided to return to Queenstown for more ropes and food. His crew were wet through and exhausted. They had had no food since the night before and had been up all night trying to save their boats. The lifeboat reached Queenstown at nine-thirty that night.

'If conditions were terrible at sea they were bad on shore. Two hours after the lifeboat had put to sea I had to go to

Cloyne, seven miles away, which was a difficult journey as the road was blocked by fallen trees. I hoped to be able to phone from there but all the lines were down. I went on to Midleton, twelve miles further on, and there found a message giving me the position of the lightship. Then I tried to reach Rochespoint, the entrance to Queenstown harbour, in the hope of getting this information to the lifeboat but fallen trees made this impossible. Returning to Midleton I telegraphed the lifeboat stations at Courtmacsherry and Youghal to tell them the Ballycotton boat was out and this time managed to get through on the telephone to Queenstown. From there I learnt that the lifeboat had been in and had put out again.

'There was nothing more to do except wait but at eleven that night as there was no news I went to Cloyne. The telephone was working once more and I was able to get through to Queenstown. I spoke to the coxswain and he told me the position. I went back at once to Ballycotton and then set out again for Queenstown with a spare drogue, drogue rope, tripping-line, veering-lines and changes of clothing for the crew. It was twenty-three miles to Queenstown and again a very difficult journey by night, dodging fallen trees. I arrived at Queenstown at three in the morning of Wednesday, 12 February, handed over the stores and returned to Ballycotton.

'Some of the crew had managed to get a little sleep but there were three men in the boat all the time, in case a call came. Early on the morning of the 12th the lifeboat set out again. As soon as she reached the lightship the *Tenedos* left but the *Isolda*, the Irish lights tender, was expected from Dublin. The wind dropped a little during this, the second day and fog set in. But the sea did not seem to go down and the lifeboat stood by all day. When the weather report was received by wireless on board the lightship at six in the evening they asked the lifeboat to continue to stand by. She stood by all night.

'At daylight next day, which was shortly after seven, the coxswain again returned to Queenstown as their petrol was getting low. They reached Queenstown at nine on the morning of the 13th after standing by for twenty-five and a half hours. The seas had been breaking continually over the crew and they had had no food.

'I had 160 gallons of petrol ready at Ballycotton but it was impossible to get a motor lorry. I telephoned Cork to send 80 gallons to the lifeboat but the driver of the lorry injured his arm and a second driver had to be found, causing some delay. As soon as the lifeboat had the petrol on board she set out again, by which time it was four o'clock in the afternoon.

'When the lifeboat reached the lightvessel again, about dusk, she found that the *Isolda* had arrived. Her captain told the coxswain that he would stand by all night and in the morning would try and take the lightship in tow. But the weather since four o'clock had been getting worse. At eight o'clock a big sea went over the lightship, carrying away the forward of the two red lights shown by a lightship out of position. At nine-thirty, with the wind and sea still increasing the coxswain took the lifeboat round the lightship's stern with his searchlight playing on her. In its light he could see her crew with their lifebelts on, huddled up at her stern. The wind, which had been south-east, had veered to south-south-east. The lightship was now not more than sixty yards from the Daunt rock, the coxswain estimated. He went to the *Isolda* and told her captain that the lightship was now in great danger. She was very near the rock, to the south-west of it, and the wind was shifting. If it went a bit west, she must strike the rock.

'The captain said that in the heavy sea it was impossible for the *Isolda* to do anything so the coxswain asked if he should try and take the crew off and was told to carry on. He took the lifeboat round the lightship again. The seas were going right over her. She was plunging tremendously on her cable, rolling from 30 to 40 degrees, burying her starboard bow in the water and throwing her stern all over the place. She was fitted with rolling chocks or bilge keels which projected over two feet from her sides and as she rolled these threshed the water.

'To anchor to windward and drop down on her was impossible owing to her anchor cable. The only thing to do was to make quick runs in on her port side, calling on her crew to jump for the lifeboat as they could. The coxswain went within hailing distance and told the lightship's crew what he intended to do. He must run in at full speed, check for a moment and then go full astern. In that second the men must jump. He knew the dangers. The lightship was only 98 feet long and if he went too far ahead the lifeboat would over-run her anchor cable and probably capsize. As he came alongside her bilge keels, threshing the water as she plunged and rolled, might crash down on top of the lifeboat.

'The coxswain went ahead of the lightship and pumped out oil to calm the seas a little but the tide was running strongly and the effect did not last long.

'He then went astern of the lightship and drove the boat at full speed alongside. One man jumped as the lifeboat went astern. Round they went again and a second time raced in alongside but nobody jumped. At the third attempt five men jumped but the fourth time the lightship sheered violently and her counter crashed down on top of the lifeboat, smashing the rails and damaging the fendering and deck. No one was hurt but the man working the searchlight sprang clear only just in time. The lifeboat went in a fifth time and again no one jumped.

'There were still two men on board the lightvessel. They were clinging to the rails and seemed unable to jump. The coxswain sent some of his crew forward where they risked being swept overboard, with orders to seize the two men as the boat came alongside. Then he drove in again for the sixth time and the survivors were quickly grabbed and dragged into the lifeboat.

'One of the men knocked his face either against the fluke of the anchor or a stanchion and was badly cut. The other man's legs were hurt. The motor mechanic was able, with iodine and bandages, to give first aid to the man whose face was cut. The long strain on the men on the lightvessel had been tremendous and shortly after the rescue one of them became hysterical and two men had to hold him down to prevent anyone from being hurt or knocked overboard.

'The lifeboat, after reporting to the *Isolde*, made for Queenstown where she arrived at eleven o'clock on the night of 13 February. The two injured men were taken to hospital. The lifeboat remained at Queenstown for the night returning next morning to Ballycotton where she arrived at a quarter to one o'clock. She had then been away from her station for 76 and a half hours. During the first and third days the weather was bitterly cold and the rain and sleet almost continuous, while the whole time the lifeboat was taking heavy seas on board.

'All the crew came back suffering from cold and salt-water burns and the coxswain had a poisoned arm. All were completely exhausted. In the 63 hours from the time they left Ballycotton until the time they brought the rescued men into Queenstown they only had three hours sleep.

'For this service Coxswain Patrick Sliney was awarded the gold medal. Second Coxswain John Walsh and Motor Mechanic Thomas Sliney the silver medal and the four other members of the crew the bronze medal. Somehow, it hardly seems enough.'

The famous Coxswain Henry Blogg of Cromer, some of whose exploits are recorded elsewhere in this book, won three gold medals. Coxswain Richard Evans of Moelfre in Anglesey won two and is the only man alive to have won more than one gold medal, so it will be seen that they are not awarded lightly.

Of the three magnificent lifeboat services which earned Henry Blogg his gold medals the most often quoted are those to the Swedish ship *Fernebo* in 1917 and to the barge *Sepoy* in 1933. Both were shining examples of the courage and determination of British lifeboatmen and of the splendid seamanship of Henry Blogg. But his other gold medal must surely be considered as having been equally well earned and indeed it would not be surprising if Blogg had thought it the most hard won of the three. It is also quite certain that he would never have ventured such an opinion to anyone.

At midnight on Sunday, 20 November 1927, the *Georgia*, a Dutch oil tanker with a cargo of crude oil from Abadan to Grangemouth, went ashore on the South Haisborough sand during a heavy gale of wind. Steering gear trouble had rendered the ship out of control and she struck the sands with such force that it broke her back and she split into two pieces. There was no time for the radio operator to put out a distress call and the after part of the vessel, which broke clear, drifted away down wind and tide leaving the fore part firmly fixed on the sandbank. There were 16 men on the after part and 15 on the forward section.

The afterpart drifted on through the wild night, battered by heavy seas and groaning and clanking as the torn hull tossed and pitched crazily. All that day she drifted with the 16 survivors holding on desperately and looking eagerly for some signs of rescue. Late in the afternoon the weary men sighted a ship and not long afterwards the steamship *Trent* got a line across to the wreck and managed to haul the survivors to safety. It could not have been an easy task and the master of the *Trent* must have been a splendid seaman to carry out the rescue with what appears to have been a minimum of fuss. The abandoned after part of the *Georgia* continued drifting and finally went ashore off Cromer. The master of the *Trent* on hearing the story of the survivors at once made for the grounded fore part of the *Georgia* and informed the coastguard that immediate assistance was required.

Flares and other distress signals from the survivors on the fore part went un-noticed in the black, blustery night and it was not until the *Trent*'s message was received that rescue work was put in hand. At 2030 on the night of Monday, 27 November, the Great Yarmouth and Gorleston lifeboat *John and Mary Meiklam* was launched and through a wild night of strong gales, high breaking seas and searching cold reached the casualty in about two hours. The survivors had now been in their precarious position for nearly 24 hours!

The *Trent* was standing by but had had no answers from the wreck and all began to wonder whether the sea had claimed the rest of the crew as victims. At dawn the *Trent* and the lifeboat endeavoured to close the wreck but with huge seas sweeping over the remains of the *Georgia* it was impossible to make contact. At noon Coxswain Fleming made another attempt to reach the wreck and used the line-throwing gun, firing four lines without success. One line actually reached the casualty but a heavy sea drove the lifeboat away and the line parted. The feelings of the stranded men may well be imagined.

At last, with some engine trouble and a cold, wet and hungry crew, Coxswain Fleming informed the master of the *Trent* that he must return to his station but would return for another attempt at daylight.

Meanwhile at Cromer Henry Blogg had discovered the wreck of the fore part four miles to the north-east of the town and had launched the lifeboat *H. F. Bailey* to investigate. He found of course that there was no one on board but in view of the possible danger to shipping of the unlit wreck he decided to stand by until daylight to warn off other vessels. It was an uncomfortable prospect with a long wild night ahead of them but Blogg never hesitated when it came to choosing between duty and comfort.

With the coming of morning the Cromer boat returned to her station to rehouse. There were now two lifeboats at

Cromer, the No. 2 boat being the *Louisa Heartwell* which had served Blogg so well in the past and which could be used to take over from the *H. F. Bailey.* Just as they were ready to put the No. 1 boat back on the slipway a report came that a man in a small boat had been sighted off Bacton so Blogg decided to investigate. He found the small boat in the surf but there was no man to be seen so once more the lifeboat returned to Cromer.

Again they were about to put the boat on the slipway ready to haul her into the boathouse but a rope fouled the propeller and the weary crew set to work to clear it. While this rather tricky operation was going on a message arrived asking for the Cromer boat to relieve the Gorleston boat at the fore part of the *Georgia,* still with 15 men on board and still fast on the Haisborough sand.

Blogg and his tired crew did not hesitate, or if they did it was but momentarily. Although they had been at sea in foul weather conditions for more than 24 hours and were sadly in need of dry clothes, food and rest they set off at once for the South Haisborough and the survivors of the *Georgia.* The Cromer No. 2 boat proceeded to the after portion of the casualty to stand by and warn shipping.

The crew of the *H. F. Bailey* are reported to have whiled away the time as the lifeboat plunged and shuddered her way south by giving vent to their feelings at the apparent lack of organisation. They had spent more than a day so far on what had proved to be something of a wild goose chase and at this stage they were inclined to guess that they were engaged on yet another abortive effort. Blogg himself was feeling the strain of his exertions and of course had no idea of what lay ahead. Suddenly his keen eye caught the dim outline of a ship. It was nearly dark and if there was work to be done it would not be easy.

There was no sign of the Gorleston boat which he expected to be standing by and as they neared the *Georgia* it was clear that the survivors must be in dire straits after their long ordeal in bitter weather. Seas were breaking high over the wreck as the men on board crouched miserably on the battered bridge. Oil from one of the fractured tanks had poured out to form a huge slick to leeward, which smothered the breaking sea into a greasy swell. Blogg saw his chance and shouted to his crew that he was going alongside. Over went the big fenders and heaving lines and warps were ready as the *H. F. Bailey* surged up to the broken hull. Almost at the moment of impact a vicious-looking sea picked up the lifeboat, spun her round and hurled her stern first against the hull of the *Georgia*, nearly washing the bowman overboard. Some damage was done but the rudder still functioned and within a minute or two Blogg had his boat alongside again. Bow and stern lines were soon fast but how long they could stand without parting as the lifeboat surged over the seas was a matter of some doubt. Encouraged by Blogg to take it steady the Dutch crew, frozen with cold and moving stiffly, nevertheless managed to leap into the lifeboat as it rose and fell giddily alongside. Members of the crew had tried to save the ship's cat and some hens without success but the cook came over the side wrapped in a Persian rug he was determined not to lose.

With the fifteen survivors safely on board the warps were cut and the Cromer lifeboat moved away with her engine roaring. But the sea had not finished with them and a huge wave, as if furious at their temerity, lifted the lifeboat high over the gunwale of the wreck. For a moment it looked like disaster but with engines going full speed astern the *H. F. Bailey* slid clear and with a quick manoeuvre her coxswain had her safe and heading for home.

The rescued men were in sorry shape after their 40 hours without food in the bitter cold and the lifeboat crew were in little better shape after a 28-hour battle with the unfriendly elements. Blogg took the boat to Gorleston as being the quickest way of bringing relief to the survivors and they all remained there for the night. Next day the *H. F. Bailey* returned to her station to be met by a great crowd of enthusiastic admirers and with the church bells ringing out a peal of welcome. Blogg's reaction is reported to have been a remark that he wished he were at home out of it.

Thus Henry Blogg won his second gold medal. All his crew were awarded bronze medals and members of the crews of the other lifeboats involved were also decorated. When the medals were presented at the RNLI annual general meeting at the Central Hall, Westminster, the then President of the Institution, HRH the Prince of Wales, made the award. He said that Blogg seemed to prefer a casualty to break in two and suggested that he should not be too particular as to the number of pieces into which vessels in distress divided themselves!

The village of Moelfre on the north coast of Anglesey has for most of its long existence remained a quiet backwater known only to its neighbours and to holidaymakers who have discovered the simple pleasures of this attractive bit of coastline. But at intervals Moelfre has leapt into prominence and hit the headlines before reverting quietly to its habitual calm existence.

From the point of view of sea rescue Moelfre's importance has stemmed from the fact that this part of the Anglesey coast, lying to the southward of Point Lynas, has always been used by vessels sheltering from gales from the south-west and to the fact that the Mersey pilots use Point Lynas for landing and embarking in their cutter. It is said that at one time it was by no means unusual to see 50 or more vessels sheltering off Moelfre. Should the wind suddenly fly round to the north or north-east when ships, especially sailing ships, were at anchor in the bay there was every likelihood that one or more would be unable to beat out to seaward and would be driven remorselessly towards the shore. When this happened the Moelfre lifeboat would be quickly into action and in its long history has never failed to answer a call for help.

Coxswain John Matthews lived almost at the water's edge and only a few yards from the lifeboathouse at Moelfre. He was coxswain for 30 or more years and possessed a lively sense of humour to reinforce his undoubted skill and courage. A lifeboat inspector making his first visit to Moelfre was somewhat taken aback to find that for the whole of the exercise not a man in the crew spoke a word of English and Matthews translated all his orders into Welsh. This went on for the whole of the exercise, the only English spoken being that used by the inspector and by Matthews to answer him.

On their way back to the lifeboat station Matthews opened out enough to give the inspector some details of the station's history and told how, in 1940, they had rescued the crew of the *Gleneden* and found they were all lascars. With an unmistakable twinkle in his eye, Matthews continued, 'Proper heathens they were, sir. Didn't speak a word of English!' Later, when another new inspector arrived to take over the district, Matthews told him, 'They always know where to find me when the lifeboat's wanted – in the chapel. I'm a deacon. The rest of the crew are just as easy to find. They'll be in the boozer!' No doubt this was rather a slanderous remark. The same inspector, hearing that Matthews was a deacon of his chapel, said that there was a very fine preacher in Holyhead and Matthews ought to get him to come and preach to them. Matthews appeared unimpressed by these remarks so the inspector proceeded to eulogise the preacher's abilities still further. Finally Matthews turned to him, again with that twinkle, and said, 'Good preacher he may be, but does he preach cheap?' You cannot go far wrong with a man like that in a lifeboat.

When he retired, Matthews was followed by another great character, Richard Evans and both of them had as motor mechanic a fine seaman and dedicated lifeboatman in Evan Owens. Together they made a magnificent team and many seamen in distress had reason to be thankful for their courage and skill.

About noon on Tuesday, 27 October 1959, the coastguard informed the Moelfre coxswain that a small vessel was dragging her anchor in Dulas bay, just north of the lifeboat station. The ship was the *Hindlea* of 506 tons, in ballast from Manchester to Newport, Monmouthshire. She had been sheltering from a south-west gale which had suddenly shifted to the northward.

Weather conditions were extreme, with the wind north by west, force 12, gusting to 104 knots with a very rough sea. Visibility was poor, reduced by flying spray and spindrift. In view of the urgency of the situation Coxswain Dick Evans decided not to wait for his usual crew to muster and launched the reserve lifeboat which was at the station with a crew of five volunteers and proceeded to the casualty.

It only took half an hour to reach the *Hindlea* which was found lying to her starboard anchor about a mile and a half north of Moelfre island. Her master was using the engines to try and ease the strain on her cable but as the vessel was in ballast and had a very light draft the propeller was racing as the ship pitched and was having very little effect. Certainly the little vessel could not have made headway against the wind and sea which was slowly but surely driving her to destruction. Even so, the master and crew stuck to their ship until it was brutally clear that nothing could save her. During this time Dick Evans kept the lifeboat just to seaward of the *Hindlea* which was yawing about violently and throwing up great sheets of spray.

About one-thirty the master of the *Hindlea* reluctantly decided that the time had come to abandon ship. He had in fact left it rather late from the lifeboat point of view. The eight members of the crew were assembled on the poop on the port side as there appeared to be slightly better conditions there for the lifeboat to come alongside. By this time the ship was getting into shallow water with the effect that the sea was a boiling mass of foam with waves seeming to run in all directions. She was now so close to the rocky shore that it looked barely possible for the lifeboat to get round her stern and come up head to wind on her port side. To Dick Evans this seemed to be the only possible way to get the survivors off the ship before she struck. When they realised what he was about to do his volunteer crew might well have wondered whether it was worth while protesting. But nobody did so and as the lifeboat plunged through the narrow gap of turbulent water between the casualty and the ever nearer shore a great wave reared up out of the blue and struck her beam on, rolling her over to an alarming angle. Terrifying as this must have been to the crew of the lifeboat it had an even greater impact on the crew of the *Hindlea* who for a few moments saw their hope of survival about to be snatched from them.

The gallant *Edmund and Mary Robinson*, doing duty while the station boat was having her annual refit, righted herself to the relief of all concerned. Still revolving ineffectively the propeller of the *Hindlea* thrashed away dangerously within feet of the lifeboat, its blades high out of the water.

There was no time to get a line aboard the casualty and even had there been it is certain that the stoutest warp would have parted as the two craft reared and plunged in the angry sea. Dick Evans brought the bow of the lifeboat up to the port quarter of the *Hindlea*, close enough for a man to jump on board and then went astern just enough to prevent his craft coming down on the gunwale of the casualty. Then ahead again and another survivor jumped to comparative safety. To some of the men it must have looked like a case of 'out of the frying pan'. Indeed at one attempt the lifeboat was driven into the side of the *Hindlea* with such force that Dick Evans thought that she must have sustained serious damage and looked anxiously to see if there were any signs of it. Fortunately there were not.

At last the eight survivors were stowed away aboard the lifeboat and the coxswain was able to take her ahead and away from the *Hindlea* which was now within yards of the shore. All landed safely at the lifeboat station soon after half past two, so the service had only taken two and a half hours. No doubt it seemed a great deal longer than that to those involved.

It was mentioned that Coxswain Evans did not wait for his regular crew on this occasion. In fact two of the men who volunteered to go with him were council roadmen and one of them had never been afloat in a lifeboat before. It must have been a rather drastic initiation!

For this splendid rescue Coxswain Dick Evans was awarded the RNLI gold medal and Motor mechanic Evan Owens the silver medal. Bronze medals were awarded to crew members D. Francis, H. Owen, and H. Jones.

In December 1966 Coxswain Richard Evans was again a leading figure in a rescue which involved both the Moelfre and the Holyhead lifeboats and which was packed with dramatic incidents. Earlier the Douglas, Isle of Man, lifeboat had also launched but was unable to locate the casualty. This was the Greek ship *Nafsiporus* of 1,287 tons which was in difficulties with engine trouble in a severe gale from the north-west, with wind speeds of over 100 knots in gusts. One report gave the wind speed as 127 knots and the sea conditions were as bad as anyone could remember. The disabled vessel was drifting rapidly towards the north coast of Anglesey.

At ten o'clock on the morning of 2 December, Holyhead coastguard informed the lifeboat honorary secretary that the *Nafsiporus* needed assistance and had given her position as 20 miles north of Point Lynas. It was agreed that the lifeboat should launch and the inspector of lifeboats for the district, Lieutenant-Commander Harold Harvey happened to arrive at the boathouse just as the coxswain was about to give the order to slip. Coxswain Thomas Alcock agreed that the inspector should join them and moments later the 52ft Barnett type lifeboat, *St Cybi – Civil Service No 9*, was sliding swiftly down the slipway to commence her turbulent journey through high, breaking seas to the estimated position of the casualty. When some 14 miles north of the Skerries a Shackleton aircraft appeared and indicated that the casualty was 12 miles to the eastward.

Moelfre lifeboat, *Watkin Williams*, had already launched earlier to escort two vessels and on receiving the report that the *Nafsiporus* needed help, also made her way to the position.

The Holyhead boat arrived on the scene three hours after launching and found the casualty with the Russian ship *Kungurles* standing by together with another vessel. The Russian ship managed to get a line aboard the Greek ship but it parted almost immediately.

The Greek seamen showed no signs of leaving their vessel and this could have been because of the antics of the lifeboats in the 20 feet high waves did not invest them with looks of either comfort or safety. Both boats stood by all afternoon as the Greek ship drifted nearer and nearer to destruction, her propeller thrashing slowly and ineffectively; quite unable to give the ship either headway or steerage way or enable her to claw off the lee shore. She was rolling heavily and with night coming on it was clear that it was going to be a highly dangerous task going alongside and taking off the crew. Shortly before four o'clock the *Nafsiporus* let go her port anchor. She was now only about a quarter of a mile off the West Mouse rock and it was unlikely that her anchor would hold her in the severe conditions obtaining. To add to the difficulties of rescue the crew of the *Nafsiporus* had endeavoured to launch one of the ship's own lifeboats and someone had let the forward fall go with a run so that the boat hung there, dangling precariously from one fall at the after end.

Nevertheless Coxswain Alcock decided to try and get alongside as it was clear that the ship was in very grave danger. As the *St Cybi* rounded the stern of the casualty the Greek ship gave a tremendous roll and yawed suddenly, crashing into the lifeboat and doing considerable damage. Alcock quickly took the *St Cybi* clear before another lurch added to the danger. It was time to take a cool look at the possibilities of effecting a rescue without endangering the lifeboat and all the lives depending on her.

The boat swinging from the davits of the *Nafsiporus* presented a problem, not only because of the fact that it left little room alongside but because of the very obvious possibility of it falling at any moment and crashing on to the deck of the lifeboat. It also meant that if the lifeboat did get alongside safely she could not stay for long and it would be necessary to grab the survivors and get them on board in very quick time. Coxswain Alcock suggested to the inspector,

Harold Harvey, that he, Alcock, should go forward and take charge on deck and that Harvey should take over the wheel. This was quickly agreed. Several attempts were made to get the Greek crew to cut the after fall of the hanging lifeboat and let it run clear but they either did not understand or did not wish to do so.

The Moelfre lifeboat stood by while the Holyhead boat made the first attempt at rescue, probably on the 'first come first served' principle. But seeing that Coxswain Alcock's first run in was unsuccessful Coxswain Dick Evans also made to come alongside. Once again the yawing of the casualty and the dangling lifeboat made the attempt abortive and in her turn the Moelfre boat had to sheer away.

Dick Evans was not to be put off for long and brought his boat round again in another and more successful effort; but the Greek crew were reluctant to leave their ship, possibly because it still appeared safer than the storm tossed lifeboats.

Then Harold Harvey brought the Holyhead boat in once more with the ship's lifeboat dangling from the after fall emphasising the need for caution. This time the Greek crew decided that the time had come to go and one man was already on the jumping ladder waiting for the lifeboat to arrive. Owing to the height of the waves the lifeboat was rising well above and below the man on the ladder and a false step would have been fatal. As the boat came up the man on the ladder was plucked aboard unceremoniously and another survivor took his place. In this manner four men were rescued and a fifth was about to be helped aboard when the lifeboat, rising high on a wave, struck the hanging ship's boat. Almost at once the remaining fall parted and down came the boat, hitting the deck of the lifeboat and crashing with a rending of timber, loud above the noise of the storm. Oars and other gear from the fallen boat were all over the place, including through the wheelhouse windows of the lifeboat. Stanchions were crushed and the lifeboatmen working on the fore deck only just managed to jump clear. Lieut-Commander Harvey had seen the danger and as the ship's boat crashed the engines were already going astern. Even so, it was a very near thing indeed, adding immediate drama to an already exciting and dangerous situation.

The ship's boat hit the deck of the lifeboat upside down. It struck the mast exhaust and bent the guard rail stanchions in all directions. In a heavy breaking sea it was the climax of a supreme test of courage, confidence and seamanship on the part of the whole lifeboat's crew. How they all escaped injury can only be explained by that overworked word 'miracle'. None of them is likely to forget that day.

But the *St Cybi* was already gathering sternway and partly due to this and partly due to a wave being helpful for once, the ship's boat rolled over and slid clear, much to everybody's relief.

The debris on deck was soon cleared but the battered ship's boat was still floating between the *St Cybi* and the *Nafsiporus*. Harvey took the Holyhead boat away to starboard to clear the wreckage and prepared to run in alongside again. In fact, this was unnecessary as Dick Evans in the Moelfre boat was standing by for just such an opportunity and within minutes was alongside the casualty with men tumbling down the ladder to be grabbed by the lifeboat crew and hauled aboard. Ten men in all were helped into the Moelfre boat leaving the Greek captain and three men still aboard the *Nafsiporus*. They had decided not to abandon ship.

Both lifeboats set course for Holyhead where they arrived at 1830. Four of the survivors who were injured were taken to hospital by a waiting ambulance. Immediately afterwards, with barely time for a cup of tea for the crew, the Holyhead boat put to sea again to stand by the *Nafsiporus* in response to a request from the Greek captain. When she arrived on the scene once more an RAF Shackleton aircraft dropped an illuminated liferaft for the casualty.

Later the Dutch tug *Utrecht* arrived and the *Nafsiporus* was taken in tow at 0700 next day, the lifeboat eventually arriving back at her station at 0800.

Not surprisingly the RNLI made a number of awards as a result of this extremely difficult and hazardous service. Lieut-Commander Harvey and Coxswain Evans were both awarded gold medals. Silver medals were awarded to Coxswain Alcock and Motor Mechanic Jones of Holyhead and to Motor Mechanic Owens of Moelfre. The other members of the crews of the two lifeboats were awarded bronze medals.

Chapter 5
The casualties of war

In time of war the task of the Royal National Lifeboat Institution of maintaining a voluntary lifeboat service becomes very much more difficult. That in the past it has not been impossible says much for the determination and humanity of those responsible for rescue organisation. In major conflicts not only are all thoughts and activities directed towards the vigorous prosecution of the war, thereby restricting the availability of men and materials for lifeboats, but a mass of wartime regulations enforced by newly appointed officials frequently limits the use of lifesaving equipment or even categorically forbids it. Usually for the best of reasons but often with the worst of results.

In 1914 the RNLI appears to have been completely unprepared for the effect of the outbreak of war on the lifeboat service. They were not alone in this unfortunate situation and the actual events seem to have occasioned no little surprise within the organisation. In the RNLI Journal of 1 February 1916 it was said,

'Of the many strange and unexpected results of this world war, none is more surprising than that it should have brought more work for the lifeboats than ever before in the history of the Institution.' This, to say the least, was surely a naïve opinion since the hazards of navigation were bound to increase with the extinction of coastal lights and removal of buoys, without considering the effects of enemy attacks on shipping. During 1916 the lifeboats were credited with the rescue of 1,185 lives, a record total for any year in their history up to that time and one that was to stand for many years.

During the war the building of lifeboats was virtually at a standstill and possibly the most far-reaching effect of this was the delay in introducing motor lifeboats, which were just coming into use at the outbreak. In fact, the war period produced such a big advance in the design and construction of internal combustion engines that in the long term the delay was not entirely a disadvantage. But with so many casualties and speed of such importance in reaching most of them the lack of power driven boats undoubtedly resulted in some lives being lost, in spite of the heroic efforts of the crews of pulling and sailing boats.

The most outstanding rescue of World War I by lifeboats was almost certainly that of the survivors of the hospital ship *Rohilla* off Whitby on 30 October 1914. She was bound for Dunkirk and had no wounded men on board but carried a crew of 229 which included five nurses. The vessel struck the Saltwick Nab in a south-east gale and soon broke into two parts. Many of those on board were swept off the after part and were drowned. The superhuman efforts to effect a rescue in almost impossible conditions emphasise the courage and determination of the lifeboat crews concerned and the vital part played by one of the earliest motor lifeboats. No less than six lifeboats were involved in the rescue attempts and of these only two had engines. The success of one of these was a clear indication of the effectiveness and future possibilities of power-driven rescue craft.

In a south-east gale the entrance to Whitby harbour can be highly dangerous and Thomas Langlands, the lifeboat coxswain, decided that conditions were too bad that day to risk trying to get clear of the piers in his No. 1 boat. He decided that the only chance of a successful launch was to haul the smaller No. 2 boat over a sea wall on skids and along the rocky foreshore to a point opposite the wreck. This was a herculean task and many people declared that it would prove impossible but with no lack of helpers the boat was eventually dragged to the piece of beach nearest to the remains of the *Rohilla*, but it was damaged in the process.

The *Rohilla* lay about a quarter of a mile from the shore on a rock-strewn shoal. Heavy seas were breaking over the wreck on the rocks and Coxswain Langlands can have had no doubts about the dangers and difficulties which had to be faced in the rescue attempt. Undismayed the crew managed to launch the lifeboat through the angry surf and nurse her over the heavy breakers and alongside the wreck. The five nurses and 12 other members of the ship's complement were taken off and landed safely. A second attempt was also successful and this time 18 people were rescued, in spite of the fact that seas were sweeping over the wreck and filling the lifeboat continuously. Unfortunately, on beaching the second time the boat was severely damaged by boulders and rendered unfit for further use.

The Upgang lifeboat, stationed north of Whitby, was promptly called out. She was sent overland on her carriage pulled by a team of horses and eventually lowered down the steep cliff on to the beach near the wreck. By this time huge seas were breaking straight on to the beach making launching impossible. All the Upgang crew could do was to stand by and await their chance. This came at daylight next morning when a successful launch was accomplished but the heavy seas breaking round the wreck were too much for the rowers and the boat could not get alongside. After many attempts the effort had to be abandoned. Hearts and muscles could do no more.

Scarborough and Teesmouth lifeboats had also been called out and the Scarborough boat reached the wreck and stood by all night in conditions of the utmost severity. Her efforts to get alongside at daylight failed as had those of the Upgang boat and for the same reason. In the shallow water surrounding the casualty the seas were breaking with such force that to approach the wreck meant almost certain disaster and it would clearly have been impossible to take survivors off. The Teesmouth lifeboat was fitted with a petrol engine but on leaving harbour she pounded so heavily that she was disabled and had to put back. When this was known the Tynemouth motor lifeboat was called and she left at once to make the 44 mile journey to Whitby, where she arrived in the early hours of Sunday, 1 November. The 50 survivors remaining in the ship had now spent two fearsome nights on the wreckage and must have been suffering severely from shock and exposure.

At daybreak Coxswain Robert Smith took the Tynemouth boat in through the breakers, round the remains of the stern of the *Rohilla* and alongside the lee side abreast the bridge structure. Enormous waves swept over the lifeboat smothering her completely and the anxious crowds watching from the shore gave a deep sigh of despair for they felt sure that she was lost. But she survived and embarked all the remaining survivors, the Captain of the *Rohilla* being the last to leave the ship. The return to harbour was made safely.

Three gold medals and four silver medals were awarded by the RNLI for this remarkable series of services. As the war was then barely three months old this might have been taken as an indication of the probable value of the lifeboat service in the ensuing years. In fact, it became more and more difficult to maintain an efficient rescue service as the war went on. Boats had to be kept on in service beyond their normal allotted span because replacements were unobtainable and the same applied to the men, some of whom were still pulling an oar in their seventies. Not surprisingly spectators found the sight of these white-haired, gnarled old men setting out in a small boat into a raging sea a very moving one.

At this time lifeboats on carriages were still drawn by horses and launching into a heavy surf was a hazardous operation, as indeed it still is today. When launching the Bridlington lifeboat on service in March 1915 a man riding one of the horses was swept off its back and drowned and two of the horses were drowned also. It was not until 1920 that the first launch using a tractor was made and the last launch using horses took place in 1934.

Many more splendid rescues were carried out during the war years of which one of the finest was by Coxswain Henry Blogg of Cromer, probably the most famous of all lifeboatmen and a man of exceptional courage and character. On 9 January 1917 the Cromer pulling and sailing lifeboat launched to the assistance of the Greek steamer *Pyrin*, at anchor in the roadstead. A north-east gale was sending in a very rough sea which was breaking heavily on the beach and on a sandbank just offshore which made launching more than ordinarily difficult. Soldiers stationed at Cromer rushed to help and with many men up to their necks in the water, lifting and pushing, the lifeboat got away. With the crew straining at the oars enough offing was gained for Blogg to be able to give the order to set sail and, going alongside the *Pyrin* he rescued her complement of 16 and landed them safely.

Hardly had the lifeboat reached the shore when a boiler explosion occurred in a Swedish ship, the *Fernebo*, which was also at anchor off Cromer. The ship at once broke into two pieces and her cargo of timber allowed the two parts to float away from one another which they did without listing or losing their trim. In spite of the fact that many of the lifeboatmen were getting on in years and clearly tired from their previous struggle through the surf the lifeboat was launched again. But this time the sea was too much for them and in the end the boat was driven back on shore. While this was happening six men from the *Fernebo* managed to get ashore in a small boat which capsized in the surf. The survivors were dragged ashore by soldiers and other spectators, led by a private in the Seaforth Highlanders.

Later in the day the two parts of the wreck drifted ashore about a mile away from one another. Attempts were made to effect a rescue by means of the rocket apparatus but although many lines were fired none reached the stern portion to which the 11 remaining survivors were clinging. Henry Blogg decided that another attempt should be made by lifeboat and at half-past nine that night she was launched again and the oarsmen once more strained every sinew to force the boat through the breakers. Watched by hundreds of spectators the lifeboat was clearly visible in the beam of a searchlight as she climbed the almost vertical face of a huge sea to disappear completely next moment as she plunged into the trough in a welter of foam. At last, with five oars broken, Blogg decided that the attempt must be abandoned and sadly the rescuers returned to the shore.

The tide had ebbed and it was now thought that there was a better chance of getting a rocket line across to the wreck but Blogg and his men were determined not to be beaten. With replacements for the broken oars the lifeboat was launched yet again and, possibly because the falling tide had reduced the surf somewhat, this time they managed to reach the wreck. Not only that but all 11 survivors were taken off and landed safely. For these gallant rescues Henry Blogg won his first gold medal; in his long and highly successful term as coxswain he won two more, a record only equalled by Sir William Hillary, the founder of the RNLI. Awards were also made to the crew and it can hardly be disputed that this recognition was well deserved yet, in spite of this and many other fine, courageous rescues carried out by lifeboatmen during the war with a total of over 4,000 lives saved, no lifeboatmen received any recognition from the state.

Almost exactly 20 years after the end of World War I Britain and France were at war with Germany again. This time the war on land made a slow, grumbling start, as if neither side was quite sure of its intentions or abilities. At sea it was quite a different matter and there was some justification for seamen feeling aggrieved at the American description of the situation as a 'phoney war'. It was extremely realistic at sea with merchant ships being sunk with great loss of life within a short time of war being declared. Apart from U-boat attacks by torpedo these same grim vessels were used to lay new and powerful magnetic mines. These had immediate success and posed great problems in the finding of counter measures.

The first lifeboat service of World War II to a victim of enemy action was carried out by the Aldeburgh lifeboat on 10 September 1939 when the *Magdapur* of Liverpool was mined off the Suffolk coast. Seventy-four survivors were landed, many of them injured by the explosion and all covered in fuel oil. It was some time before the stains of oil and blood on the boat ceased to remind the crew of the perils of war.

At the beginning of October 1939, a month after the start of the war, two large vessels were mined in the Bristol channel near Swansea. Both were abandoned by their crews who took to their boats no doubt under the impression that they had been torpedoed and that the U-boat was at hand to finish off their ships if necessary. One vessel, the *Marwarri*, belonged to the Brocklebank line and had a lascar crew, some of whom were injured by the explosion. They were lucky to be saved as their boats were spotted by the examination vessel in thick weather just as they were about to drive ashore near Mumbles head. They were landed by the Mumbles lifeboat in her first service of the war.

The other vessel was the *Lochgoil* of the Royal Mail line and she was mined the following day. Her crew, after taking to the boats, were picked up by another ship and landed safely. Her captain was badly injured by the explosion which severely damaged the ship. Both these vessels were beached in Swansea bay and subsequently repaired, returning to duty at a time when every merchant ship was urgently needed. Later in the war Coxswain William Gammon and his crew carried out a brilliant service to the Canadian frigate *Cheboque* as she was driving ashore in Mumbles bay in a full gale. They rescued 42 men and for this determined and courageous service Gammon was awarded the gold medal of the RNLI. As has been told, Gammon and his crew all lost their lives in a rescue attempt shortly after the war.

During the seven months of the 'phoney' war the fearful total of 135 British merchant ships and 143 neutral ships were sunk and from them 794 merchant seamen lost their lives. At sea at least there was no doubt about the reality of the war. For the British lifeboatmen there was little time to consider the niceties of descriptions. The war was upon them with unparalleled ferocity, making tremendous demands on their courage, determination and seamanship. The winter months of 1939–40 were particularly severe with temperatures well below freezing for weeks on end. The first seven months of the war produced more casualties than ever before in the history of the RNLI and for each of four months the figures for lives saved were higher than in a normal peacetime year. Fortunately the fearful loss of ships and men did not continue at the same rate. As more naval escorts became available for convoys and more minesweepers were commissioned to increase the sweeping programmes the toll was reduced. Possibly those who predicted that there would be no war and insisted that re-arming was unnecessary felt some pangs of conscience at the loss of so many brave seamen.

Seamen in general and lifeboatmen in particular not only had to contend with the results of relentless enemy action but also with the additional hazards of bad weather and lack of lighted navigation marks at night. The honorary secretary of the Walmer lifeboat station wrote in a report that:

'The sea is dotted with sunken vessels, unbuoyed and unlit, and on moonless or overcast nights the men are without assistance to safety during their passages, other than their trust in God and their own stout hearts.'

It must be remembered, too, that at this time lifeboats carried nothing in the way of aids to navigation other than a compass and a leadline. Precisely the same equipment as would have been available hundreds of years previously.

Whereas in peacetime the authority to launch a lifeboat is in the hands of the honorary secretary of the station, during the war permission had to be sought from the naval officer in charge (NOIC) of the district in which the boat operated. Not only that, in the early days of the war the NOIC assumed complete control and gave orders for the boat to launch. These orders were not always backed by sufficient knowledge of lifeboat methods and were sometimes attended by unsatisfactory results. Fortunately the navy saw the force of the suggestion that the RNLI, their officers, coxswains and crews, were fully experienced in the demands of rescue work and that the decision to launch must be theirs, subject to permission being granted by the NOIC. This worked better than the original system but still caused tremendous frustration when permission to launch was refused or delayed. In more than one instance lifeboatmen felt that lives were lost due to delays in getting permission and because of conflicting changes of orders. Possibly there were special considerations of which they were not aware but it was galling to see a fishing boat sent out to do a lifeboat's work as sometimes happened. But that of course is war, and 'the proper channels' are usually tortuous and restricted.

One example will be enough to illustrate the 'pull devil, pull baker' conditions under which lifeboatmen had to carry out their work of rescue in wartime. At Fleetwood in 1941 an auxiliary schooner from the Faroe islands had been instructed by the examination vessel to anchor when she arrived at night in bad weather. Soon after dawn her cable parted and she began to drift towards one of the many shoals in the vicinity. The lifeboat crew had assembled and waited impatiently in the boathouse for the necessary permission to launch. In the meantime the examination vessel endeavoured to take the schooner in tow but the towrope parted and the casualty drifted once more towards the shoals. By now the weather had worsened considerably and it was clear that the vessel was in great danger. What might have been a straightforward rescue in the early stages was rapidly becoming a difficult and dangerous one. Permission for the lifeboat to launch was given and then withdrawn almost immediately. Twice this happened, by which time the lifeboatmen were no doubt using some of the more pungent seafaring expressions to describe those in authority. From the position of the casualty it was clear that the time was fast approaching when their resolute efforts might well prove of little use.

Once more permission to launch was given and this time the boat was away too quickly for any countermand to be effective. Possibly in a modern equivalent of Nelson's blind eye the telephone receiver had been left off the hook. Once afloat the coxswain drove the boat into the gale lashed seas at full speed so that she was washing down fore and aft and throwing up great sheets of spray. Those on shore had no difficulty in following her progress although they rarely glimpsed the boat herself.

The schooner had now struck the shoal and was being driven by the waves hard up on to a bank, her crew clinging desperately to the rigging. The seas broke in thunderous crashes on her weather side and swept relentlessly over her decks. The lifeboat coxswain knew that there was no time for a cautious approach and ran straight into the shallows and alongside the wreck. A heavy sea slewed the stern of the lifeboat against the casualty and damaged her rudder but somehow they managed to stay alongside long enough for the survivors to jump aboard or be dragged across by the lifeboatmen. It was literally not a moment too soon. Had there been one more delay, lives would almost certainly have been lost in the turbulent seas across the shoals. No doubt there were good reasons for the decisions of the naval authority and this account only gives the point of view of the lifeboat crew. Nevertheless, it gives a reasonably fair idea of some of the additional difficulties faced by the sea rescue service in Britain during the war.

While it is probable that the naval authorities were guided principally by consideration for the safety of the lifeboat and her crew their orders did not always operate to that end. In December 1941 the navy asked for the Minehead lifeboat to be launched to investigate a floating object in the bay but the coxswain discussed the matter with the honorary secretary and decided to take his own boat. The shore signalman of the station went with him and they were seen to reach the object. A moment later there was a loud explosion and the boat and the two men were blown to pieces. Had the lifeboat been sent it is probable that another five men would have lost their lives and a valuable rescue craft would have been destroyed also.

During the Battle of Britain the skies were full of planes and, it must have seemed to lifeboatmen, the seas full of shot-down airmen. The air-sea rescue service with its fast craft was the first line of defence with seaplanes and a number of other rescue devices in addition. Later came the airborne lifeboat, parachuted down to survivors in rubber dinghies, but in spite of the extensive organisation designed to save every airman possible the lifeboats still managed to find plenty of useful and encouraging work to do, if only in a stopgap capacity. As happened much later when helicopters came into service, lifeboat crews lived very frustrating lives being beaten to the casualty by much faster air-sea rescue craft time after time. It says much for the determination and character of these men that they still continued to turn out to search for airmen down in the sea, whatever the weather and knowing quite well that the probability was that they would have nothing to show for their efforts. A long search in bad weather is one of the most wearying of lifeboat tasks and deeply depressing if it proves unsuccessful. In fact, out of 1,050 launches to search for airmen, lifeboats were credited with the rescue of 142 men.

The general alert for lifeboat crews came as an official message 'Expect air battle in this area within the hour. Lifeboat stand by'. On one such occasion the Weymouth lifeboat put to sea to search for a vessel which had been bombed and an aircraft reported to have crashed. An aerial battle was in progress overhead and fragments of metal were whistling down and splashing into the sea all round. To crown all a German aircraft came hurtling through the air and crashed into the waves only a few yards from the lifeboat. The plane sank almost at once but one member of its crew was rescued in a parlous condition. He was the first German airman rescued by the RNLI. Others followed and the RNLI was angrily taken to task for saving them by those who condemned the Germans for their indiscriminate bombing. Of course the lifeboats continued to save friend and foe alike and in this the essential humanity of the lifeboat crews was impressively emphasised, since they and their families were no strangers to enemy bombing, either.

On 30 May 1940 the Ministry of Shipping asked the RNLI to send as many lifeboats as possible to Dover at once. No doubt it was inevitable that lifeboats should become involved in the evacuation of the British army from Dunkirk but in view of their special position in international law there can be no doubt that they should not have been used for this purpose, except possibly to remove wounded troops. There was some evidence that the lifeboats of occupied countries had been used for what might be considered military purposes, which could be said to justify the use. At least it was quite understandable.

Only two lifeboats crossed the channel manned by their

own crews; the remaining 17 which went to Dover were taken over by naval crews after a sturdily independent RNLI coxswain had queried his position as a non-combatant and also his instructions for operating on the beaches, which he considered unworkable. The Margate and Ramsgate lifeboats had sailed direct to Dunkirk so did not become involved with the naval authorities at Dover. Both boats did splendid work, ferrying the battle-worn troops from the beaches to vessels lying off-shore in deep water, often under shell fire or bombing attack. The Ramsgate lifeboat *Prudential* under Coxswain Howard Primrose Knight and *The Lord Southborough* of Margate under Coxswain Edward Drake Parker returned safely to their stations eventually with their crews completely exhausted, since rest in the boats was impossible. Both coxswains were subsequently awarded the Distinguished Service Medal for their gallantry and determination.

There was great disappointment that the other lifeboats were not allowed to operate with their own crews but in fact as they had now been requisitioned by the navy the use to which they were put subsequently was presumably quite in order. The RNLI personnel did sterling work at Dover training naval stokers to run the engines and carrying out maintenance duties, although most of them were probably convinced that they would have been better employed actually running the boats.

During the period of the war RNLI lifeboats rescued 6,376 lives, which was more than in the previous 18 years of peace. Of this number, 1,350 were men of foreign nations. People at home and abroad gave generously to the funds of the RNLI but one particular legacy touched the heartstrings of all who knew. In November 1940 the armed merchant-cruiser *Jervis Bay* was escorting a convoy in the Atlantic when it was attacked by a German pocket battleship. *Jervis Bay* engaged her formidable opponent in what all must have known was a heroic sacrifice and sank with her guns still firing. Two months afterwards the Admiralty told the RNLI that her crew had decided that should the ship be lost, half her mess funds should go to the lifeboat service. There could be no greater tribute.

Chapter 6

Aground on the Goodwin sands

The Goodwin sands lie some three or four miles off the east coast of Kent and stretch roughly from Ramsgate to St Margaret's bay, south of Walmer. They are reputed to have been part of the estate of the Saxon warrior Godwin, Earl of Wessex, until they were overwhelmed by the sea. For seamen they have borne a reputation for acute hostility to ships from the earliest days and it is rare for any vessel which goes aground on the Goodwins to get off again. The sands appear to have a peculiarly adhesive property and are loath to let go of their prey. A combination of confused seas, unpredictable currents and treacherous sands almost invariably make salvage impossible. The number of masts and bits of wreckage still showing above the sands bear witness to the many victims of this maritime trap and should be a warning to the unwary.

All ships leaving the port of London for the southward must pass the Goodwins, either by the inner channel leading to the Downs off Deal or by going the long way round outside the sands. Most large vessels prefer the long way rather than navigate the comparatively narrow inner channel. Ships from the continent making for the Dover strait must pass close to the eastern side of the sands and strangely enough it has usually been the ships taking the 'safe' outside route that have managed to strike the sands. It should be emphasised that the sands are well marked with lightships on the north, east and south sides and with numerous light buoys. Both the Ramsgate and Walmer lifeboats have rescued many people from ships on the Goodwins and the Dover boat has also been called upon on a number of occasions.

This part of the coast has bred many fine inshore seamen and indeed at one time they had the reputation for practising many clever but not always entirely legal ways of earning a living from the sea. But they also had a reputation for being prepared to risk everything to save lives of seamen in danger and this reputation remains untarnished to this day.

The Deal boatmen or hovellers as they were called were known by seamen all over the world for the skill and daring with which they handled their great luggers. These were huge open boats up to 40 feet in length and designed to launch through the heavy surf which an onshore gale flung on the beaches. Haul-off warps, anchored to a heavy mooring well off shore, were used to force the boats through the breaking seas which would have defied any other method of getting a boat afloat.

The term hoveller or hobbler was, and probably still is used all round the coasts of Britain and is certainly met with in the Isle of Man. The origin is uncertain but the word has generally been used to describe a man who makes his living along the shore. Although undoubtedly used to describe quite ordinary, decent folk, the term has also been used in a very uncomplimentary way.

The Deal boatmen made their living by rendering a variety of services to the many ships which for one reason or another brought up in the Downs or were passing through. Taking the master aboard an outward bound ship was a common undertaking as many captains avoided the tow down river from the London docks and often stayed in lodgings in Deal while their vessels were weatherbound, waiting for a favourable wind down channel. Nelson was more than once put aboard his ship here and appreciated the skill of the boatmen.

Another lucrative source of business was salvage and one elderly hoveller described how his grandfather once sat at a table by the beach with piles of golden sovereigns stacked neatly before him. He wore a black broadcloth suit and a hard hat and might easily have been taken for a parson. The men of his crew presented their hats for their share and on more than one occasion the salvage money amounted to £100 a man. Real money in those days but not earned without terrifying risks and discomfort.

The difficulties facing the old pulling and sailing lifeboats can hardly be exaggerated but there is reason to believe that although their methods of propulsion were unsophisticated these boats had more life and feeling in them than have those powered by internal combustion engines. Something of the mutual reliance that man and horse can acquire but which can hardly be achieved by the driver and his motor car. Anyone who has handled small craft will understand. Even so, it must have been salutary for the captain of a fine big steamer in trouble to see the lifeboat approaching, thrashing through an angry sea and heeled over gunwale awash, under a press of sail. Yet it was over a hundred years after the advent of steam before a British lifeboat had power propulsion.

An instance of a sailing lifeboat going to the assistance of a steamer occurred in December 1872 when the Italian ship *Sorrento* drove ashore on the Goodwins in a south-west gale. Her distress signals were seen and heard at Walmer and Kingsdown at half-past two in the morning and the bell summoning the Walmer crew clanged its urgent message over the roar of the gale. At Kingsdown the crew had to be knocked up by a runner who hammered on their doors as he pounded round the village.

Both boats launched and in those days of primitive communications, they met off-shore so that the coxswains could agree a plan of action.

Jarvist Arnold in the Kingsdown boat made for the southern end of the Goodwins where the seas in a gale run high and steep but he negotiated them safely and shortly came up with the stranded steamer. A red flare was lit according to the pre-arranged plan and the Walmer lifeboat at once made for the spot.

When the *Sorrento* struck at midnight she was drawing 21 feet of water but by the time the Kingsdown boat reached her she was hard and fast in a mere six feet. The Kingsdown coxswain put 14 men aboard the steamer, some from his own crew and some from the Walmer boat, to assist the Italians in jettisoning cargo to lighten the ship as much as possible. This soon proved to be useless as the *Sorrento* had broken her back and was taking in water rapidly.

By eleven o'clock next morning it was clear that there was no hope of saving the ship and seas were breaking over her fore and aft. There was no other course now but to abandon ship and the master of the *Sorrento* decided that the lifeboats would not be able to carry all his crew so he signalled for more help. It would seem that this signal was never seen for no help came. With the rising tide the weather worsened and the decks of the casualty were being swept clean. Her crew retired to the upper bridge as the only part reasonably dry and waited for an opportunity to board the lifeboats.

Just then a huge sea struck the unlucky vessel, carrying away her own lifeboats and parting the Walmer boat's mooring rope which held her alongside. The lifeboat crashed into the tangle of wreckage and had a hole knocked in her hull by the *Sorrento*'s anchor. The eight men remaining in the lifeboat hung on for dear life as she spun round in the vicious seas and drifted away. She had travelled half a mile before the crew were able to let go an anchor and bring her up.

On board the *Sorrento* there were 46 men. Thirty-two crew members and the 14 lifeboatmen. Now there was only one small lifeboat to take them on board as it was clear that the Walmer boat would not be able to make her way back to the ship.

Jarvist Arnold realised that he had a difficult task on his hands. Forty-six men had to be carried ashore safely in one small open boat. Three of the men concerned were his own sons who had boarded the *Sorrento* to help jettison cargo. The Kingsdown lifeboat lay to an anchor some little distance from the casualty and with the strong current now running Arnold knew that if he weighed there was a strong possibility that his remaining crew would not be able to pull the boat alongside. They might well be swept away to leeward like the Walmer boat.

So the coxswain ordered the spare anchor warp to be bent on to the one in use and with all the men pulling oars on one side he managed to veer the lifeboat over towards the *Sorrento*. Just as it looked as if the manoeuvre had been successful the bowman sang out that they were on the bitter end of the second warp and he could veer no more. All this time seas were breaking over the lifeboat, filling her to the gunwales so that the crew had to hold on for their lives to avoid being washed overboard.

Suddenly, one of the men on board the *Sorrento*, possibly one of the lifeboatmen, realised what had happened and bending a leadline on to a cork fender he threw the fender over the side in an attempt to veer it down to the lifeboat. At first he was unsuccessful as the fender seemed determined to go any way except towards the lifeboat, until a fortunate eddy caught it and swept it in the right direction. Men's lives depended on this simple trick of fate. Quickly one of the lifeboat crew grabbed the line with a boathook and bent on a heavier rope which was hauled aboard the *Sorrento* and made fast. With her crew all hauling on the rope together the lifeboat was inched towards the casualty and finally lay alongside.

A man jumped from the steamer but missed the lifeboat and fell in the sea but was quickly seized and hauled aboard. One after another the whole 46 men jumped or slid down ropes and were dragged into the lifeboat. By the time the last man was aboard space must have been at a premium as there were now 54 men in the gallant little craft and she cannot have had much freeboard. Sails were hoisted and she shot away from the wreck which promptly broke in two, soon to disappear almost entirely into the hungry sands.

With his heavy load and small freeboard Arnold was strictly limited in how he handled the boat and at first could only run down wind, which was in fact taking him further from the shore. But the Walmer boat, now under sail herself, made up towards them, no doubt with a view to collecting her own crew members and relieving the Kingsdown boat of some of the survivors. In the confused sea the two boats came together with a crash as with a minimum of ceremony the transfer took place and both headed for the shore. All the survivors were landed safely.

There were many fine rescues carried out on the Goodwin sands by the pulling and sailing lifeboats and one cannot but have unbounded admiration for the skill and courage of the men responsible. Much as the world has changed, the sands still claim their victims and skill and courage are still necessary to carry out the work of rescue.

A fine rescue under difficult and dangerous conditions was carried out by the Walmer lifeboat under her famous coxswain, Freddie Upton, in 1948. On the afternoon of 2 January the Deal coastguard informed Mr Shelvey, honorary secretary of the Walmer station, that a ship appeared to have gone aground on the Goodwin sands about a mile and a half west of the East Goodwin lightvessel. Mr Shelvey agreed to launch and told the coxswain with the result that within ten minutes the lifeboat *Charles Dibdin Civil Service No 2* went sliding down the beach from her launching cradle and smacked into the sea in a smother of spray. It was then high tide with a moderate south-west wind and a moderate sea. The visibility was poor with mist and rain.

As it was high tide the coxswain took a short cut right across the middle of the sands which, although it was not blowing hard, were covered with a short, confused sea which seemed to come from all directions at once. In an hour the lifeboat was alongside the stranded ship which proved to be the Italian steamer *Silvia Onorato*, bound from the Adriatic to Rotterdam. She was aground aft on the extreme edge of the sands on the east side and here much heavier seas were breaking over her and slewing her bow from side to side.

In his first attempt to get alongside the coxswain approached cautiously because of the movement of the ship but a big sea swept under the stern of the lifeboat lifting her high above the deck of the casualty so that the lifeboatmen found themselves looking down on her hatches. For a moment it looked as if the lifeboat would strike the gunwale of the ship and capsize but Coxswain Upton had already foreseen the danger and swung the boat clear.

Having avoided this danger Upton changed his plan and steered round the stern of the vessel and alongside the other side where a rope ladder had been thrown over. Ginger Thomas, one of the lifeboatmen, scrambled up the ladder and boarded the ship. He was met by her captain who asked what could be done to get the ship off. Thomas, who knew the Goodwin sands as well as anyone, realised that there was a ridge of sand between the vessel and deep water. He advised the captain to go ahead at full speed with the helm hard over. In this way he hoped to drive the ship over the ridge but she moved ahead only to strike again with a jar which made the whole vessel shudder. By now the tide had fallen and there was only about 14 feet under her and she drew over 18.

The wind and sea were increasing and it was clear that the lifeboat could not remain alongside but would have to lie off in deeper water. The captain was told that the lifeboat would stand by and if he fired a rocket for assistance she would return at once. Thomas returned to the boat which anchored in deep water about a mile away and set a watch to keep an eye on the steamer. A tot of rum was issued to the crew who were now cold and wet as they settled down for their night's vigil.

At 0130 the lifeboat weighed anchor and closed the

steamer. It was too rough for her to get alongside so for the next five hours she 'dodged' round the casualty. There was no sign of the vessel moving at high water and Upton asked the captain if he would abandon ship. He refused to do so and Upton said he would have to return to Walmer to refuel but would come out again and continue to stand by.

The lifeboat reached Walmer about 0800 and the crew had a welcome break ashore to get into dry clothes and snatch a meal. The shore helpers, many of whom had stood by all night ready to bring the boat ashore, refuelled her and she left again in half an hour.

At 0930 she was again close to the casualty and anchored half a mile away awaiting high tide. Now a dense mist came up and they lost sight of the steamer for a time. So the morning passed and in the afternoon the lifeboat weighed anchor once more and went alongside the casualty. The captain insisted that the ship was in no danger and said that he and the crew would remain on board. Tugs had arrived but could not get near enough to get lines aboard and it was too rough for the lifeboat to run them.

The mist had cleared and with a rising wind and sea the situation looked far from promising. As dusk fell Upton told the captain that it would be impossible to get alongside before morning but again he refused to leave his ship. No doubt with a philisophical shrug of his shoulders, Upton took the lifeboat about a mile away and anchored once more. It was now blowing a full gale with a high, breaking sea. The crew were very cold and faced with another night's vigil in acute discomfort. It should be pointed out here that the *Charles Dibdin* was an open boat with no cabin and only a small canopy aft to protect the mechanics and the helmsman. With sheets of spray flying over the boat and occasionally shipping solid water as she plunged down into a trough, it was very difficult to keep dry, even in oilskins and seaboots.

At daybreak on Sunday the lifeboat weighed and made her way over the sand through a madly confused sea to where the *Silvia Onorato* still lay. Freddie Upton once more tried to persuade the captain to abandon ship for, as he pointed out, once the tide ebbed he would not be able to reach them until the afternoon. The captain still refused to leave his ship and no members of the crew showed signs of wishing to do so. Upton told the captain that he proposed to return to Walmer for rest and refreshment as by the time they got ashore they would already have spent some 42 hours afloat. He also told him to call North Foreland radio if he needed assistance and the lifeboat would return immediately. With that they left, heading across the sands over which a typical Goodwins sea was tumbling viciously. As usual when cutting across the sands, Upton hoped that they would not strike a bit of submerged wreckage or the fluke of an old anchor.

On reaching Walmer the boat was hauled out on to her turntable and swung seawards, ready for immediate launching. Fresh supplies of rum, biscuits and chocolate were placed on board while the crew went home to get some food, rest and dry clothes before setting out again that afternoon.

About three o'clock the *Charles Dibdin* launched once more and arrived at the *Silvia Onorato* an hour and a half later. This time the coxswain decided to go on board himself to try and persuade the captain to abandon ship, as he was sure she would never leave the sands now. He was met by an Alsatian dog, which he said was the most frightening part of the whole service. But the dog proved to be friendly and indeed kept calm and good tempered throughout the whole affair.

When Upton explained the position to the captain he hesitated and sent for his chief engineer. The engineer said he saw no reason why they should abandon ship as she was not leaking and appeared to be in little danger at present. Upton pointed to the wreckage dotted about the sands and said it was very rare for a ship to get off again after being so long in the grip of the sands. But the captain was still determined to stick by his ship so Upton said he would anchor as close as he could and stand by her. Just as Upton was leaving the ship a message was received from Lloyds' agents at Dover saying that a south-west gale was imminent with gusts up to 50 miles an hour.

This was all that was necessary to convince the captain that the coxswain's advice was sound and he agreed to abandon ship. There was a big sea running and conditions alongside the casualty were decidedly unpleasant. It needed all Upton's skill to keep the lifeboat in position as one by one 28 Italians, two German stowaways and the Alsatian dog scrambled down the ladder and jumped aboard, assisted by the lifeboatmen. The crew of the lifeboat must have been very relieved to see the survivors on board their craft at last for it had looked very much as if they were destined to spend yet a third night off the sands, lying to an anchor in acute discomfort.

By half past five the rescue was completed and Upton sent a radio message to say that they were returning with all survivors on board. Fifty-one hours had passed since the boat was first launched to the assistance of the *Silvia Onorato*, most of which had been spent at sea in vile weather conditions and often in a difficult and dangerous situation over the sands themselves.

For this fine service the RNLI awarded the silver medal to Coxswain Upton, the bronze medal to mechanic Percy Cavell and the Thanks on Vellum to the remainder of the crew.

A complete history of all the wrecks which have occurred on the Goodwin sands would make very interesting reading and fill a large number of volumes. It is likely that there are many superstitions and stories of the supernatural connected with this graveyard of fine ships and there must have been many a master who could only explain how he came to lose his ship by suggesting some evil influence emanating from the sands themselves, claiming sacrificial victims to satisfy some strange rite. It may indeed have seemed like that to the unhappy mariners but there is no doubt that in many cases faulty navigation must have been the cause.

In the case of the French steamer *Agen* the cause of her stranding is not known but the result was in no doubt whatever for she broke in two almost immediately after hitting the sands.

On the night of 13 January 1952 the coastguard informed Walmer lifeboat station that the *Agen*, a ship of 4,000 tons, had sent a wireless message that she was aground on the South Goodwin and needed assistance. She was bound from Dakar to Hamburg.

Soon after eleven o'clock the lifeboat *Charles Dibdin, Civil Service No 2* was launched. As her name suggests she was the gift of the Civil Service Lifeboat Fund as were, and are, a considerable number of other RNLI lifeboats.

It was a pitch black night with heavy rain squalls and poor visibility. There was a gale from the south-west putting up a very heavy sea. It was, perhaps, typical lifeboat weather. Not at all the sort of night to leave a nice warm bed for a cold, wet lifeboat.

Coxswain Upton made for the South Goodwins and had

just sighted the lightvessel when a message was received by radio telephone that the *Agen* was in fact six miles to the north-east of the position originally given. Conditions on the sand were now very bad indeed so Upton set a course along their western edge. Arrived at the new position there was no sign of the casualty, in spite of the fact that visibility had improved. Failing any other information Upton decided to retrace his course and after travelling for about two miles a red flare was sighted on the port beam. But it was on the other side of the sands and in the existing conditions it would have been foolhardy to attempt to cross them. Upton was able to judge to a nicety when one could or could not get across the sands and on this occasion he was in no doubt at all. He took the lifeboat right down to the southern end of the sands and up the eastern side. This increased the distance by four miles but at least made sure of reaching the casualty.

It was 0245 on the morning of 14 January when the lifeboat reached the *Agen* and saw that the unfortunate vessel was in two parts with about 30 feet of angry water between them. In the light of the searchlight it could also be seen that what appeared to be the whole of the vessel's crew were clustered on the forward section. This lay about a quarter of a mile away from the remains of three other vessels which had met a similar fate and from which the Walmer lifeboat had rescued the crews, 115 men in all, during the last six years. Close to the *Agen* on her north and west sides were sandbanks which were barely covered with water and the tide was ebbing rapidly.

The situation may well be imagined. A dark night, a heavy confused sea and the broken portions of the ship with jagged steel plates ready to tear and maim the lifeboat and her crew. The coxswain made several attempts to get alongside and stay there long enough for the survivors to jump aboard but conditions were all against him and he decided that he must wait until they improved.

Soon after three o'clock the wind moderated somewhat and veered to the northward and a couple of hours later Upton decided on another attempt. It was now low water and the banks to the north and west acted to some extent as a breakwater. But it was still pitch dark and a nasty steep sea was running.

Summing up the situation the coxswain decided that he must try and get alongside the other side of the wreck. The only way to do that was to run between the two broken sections of the *Agen*, hoping that the lifeboat would not be forced on to one of the jagged ends. Luck was on his side and Upton took his boat through the gap and alongside the forward section. By using rapid engine movements he was able to keep the lifeboat in position long enough for 37 Frenchmen to slide down ropes into her. One man missed the lifeboat and was injured in the fall but the crew hauled him aboard. The French captain refused to leave his ship, in spite of the fact that she was in two pieces and could not possibly be saved.

The lifeboat was now in a sort of trap as she could not go ahead because of the sandbanks and the only thing to do was to come out through the jagged gap stern first. This was safely accomplished and Upton again asked the captain to leave the ship but he refused. As some of the rescued men were showing signs of distress the coxswain decided that he must land them so the boat headed away for Walmer to do so. Returning to the *Agen* Upton once more tried to persuade the captain to leave, pointing out the hopelessness of his position but each time he waved the lifeboat away. Eventually however he realised that there was indeed no hope for the ship and sadly jumped for the lifeboat as Upton brought her up alongside. Again there was the nerve-wracking passage through the gap but the boat came through safely and returned to Walmer arriving just after ten o'clock.

For this difficult and hazardous service Coxswain Fred Upton was awarded a bar to his silver medal and Percy Cavell a bar to his bronze medal. Other awards were made by the RNLI and the French Lifeboat Society to all members of the crew.

There are many, many stories of fine rescues following the loss of a stout ship on the Goodwin sands and in spite of the brilliant modern aids to navigation in all probability there will be more. But the lifeboatmen of Ramsgate, Walmer and Dover will undoubtedly be just as willing and able to render assistance to mariners in difficulties in the future as they are today and always have been.

Chapter 7

Some strange incidents

The rescue services are sometimes involved in very unusual situations and even if not engaged in rendering assistance are concerned with many strange happenings at sea.

What was perhaps one of the most macabre began with a report from a lightship that a man had passed them in a small rowing boat and had refused offers of assistance. Apparently he said that he was quite all right and rowed away steadily. He was a long way from land and was heading seawards. Some time later a further report was received from a ship to the effect that they had picked up a boat with a man's body in it. He had been shot through the head. Presumably it was a case of suicide but by what strange process of unreason he had decided to row miles out to sea before ending his life must remain for ever a mystery.

Another unusual incident followed a report that a motor cruiser was in distress in the Straits of Dover. The rescue services were alerted but shortly afterwards a ship reported that they had picked up the sole occupant of the cruiser and that they had found him in a large rubber dinghy filled with antiques! Whether this led to any further developments when the survivor and his unusual but possibly valuable cargo was landed is not known.

Some years ago the St David's, Pembrokeshire, lifeboat was involved in a smart and particularly rewarding rescue. One of the local farmers owned a light aircraft which he piloted himself, using a field adjacent to his farmhouse as a landing ground. On one occasion the assistant mechanic of the lifeboat was flying with him and on returning the aircraft circled the farmhouse as usual and then headed out to sea apparently to make a landing approach. The farmer's wife heard the plane circling and a few minutes later realised that it had not returned to make its landing. She remembered that her husband had told her that if after circling the farmhouse the plane had not come in to land within five minutes she was to alert the lifeboat. She at once rang Dr Soar, the honorary secretary of the station, who gave orders for the boat to launch immediately and make a search along the line of the landing approach.

Within minutes the lifeboat was sliding down the slipway into Ramsey sound and at full speed made for the other side of the island. Some distance beyond the island was a rock and clinging to it the lifeboatmen found their assistant mechanic Gwilym and the farmer, neither of whom could have held on much longer in those turbulent waters. It was a very happy end to what would certainly have been a fatal accident had not the farmer's wife acted so promptly and intelligently.

Many of the inhabitants of the Orkney islands are tough farmer-seafarers who think nothing of ferrying a boatload of sheep from island to island, not always in the best of weather and sheep make a very unreliable crew. So the Stronsay secretary was not entirely surprised when he received a message from the coastguard to say that a man was adrift in a dinghy off Noup head on the island of Westray. This was at 1010 on 18 June 1962 and the message went on to say that the weather was bad with a south-east wind approaching gale force and a rough sea which did not seem to offer much hope for the man in the dinghy.

At 1040 the Stronsay lifeboat *John Gellatly Hyndman* put to sea on the flood tide. Further reports reached the lifeboat while on her way to the position given and at 1300 the boat was sighted with the occupant still safe and sound. Half an hour later the man and his dinghy were on board the lifeboat which had set a course for Pierowall on the island of Westray.

The rescued man proved to be William Fergus, aged 71, and he informed the lifeboat crew that he was very glad to see them but he had already prepared himself for the end. In fact this might be taken as a classic example of the rescue services functioning without fuss and in an entirely efficient manner, from the original sighting of the lone fisherman to the subsequent rescue by lifeboat with the minimum loss of time. Indeed, to round off the incident, on landing at Pierowall the ladies of the Westray Lifeboat Guild were ready and waiting with a substantial tea for the survivor and his rescuers.

Although it is unlikely that strange and unusual services will lead to the award of medals for the lifeboatmen involved there is often an element of humour which at least helps to compensate for some of the time and effort expended. One such service occurred at a northern lifeboat station when a report that a small boat was missing from its berth on the beach raised the possibility that someone might have taken it to sea in the rough weather prevailing. As it was also reported that a patient was missing from a nearby mental home there was also the chance that the two facts might be connected. Instructions were given for a search to be made and on a rather unpleasant winter's day, late in the afternoon, the maroons summoning the lifeboat crew were fired.

Realising that there was very little daylight left the coxswain was anxious to get away and as he was one short in the crew he accepted the offer of a sturdy looking bystander to take the place in the boat. The launch went off without difficulty and the lifeboat searched until dark without finding a trace of the missing craft. After a time it was decided that there was no possibility of success in the dark and the weather conditions experienced and the lifeboat was recalled with instructions that the search should be resumed at daylight.

As the crew disembarked and were removing their lifebelts and oilskins an ambulance with two attendants from the mental home were waiting in the hope that their missing patient had been recovered. As the stranger who had volunteered removed his protective clothing one of the attendants cried, 'There's our missing patient. Come on, Joe, we have come to take you home.'

As he turned to leave, Joe quietly asked the coxswain what they had been searching for and on being told that someone had taken a boat off the beach, he remarked, 'Nobody but a bloody madman would go to sea on a night like this,' and departed with his keepers.

At Rhyl in north Wales some years ago the lifeboat carried out a most successful service which might well come within the scope of the description 'a great rescue'. Two young boys, about seven and ten years of age, were carried out to sea on a rubber raft or dinghy and by the time the alarm reached the lifeboat and she had launched there was no sign of the boys or the dinghy off the beach. The coxswain considered the probable direction of drift and proceeded to make a search. The visibility was not good and the light was failing so that the chances of finding and rescuing the two lads began to grow slim. Nothing but grey, misty sea surrounded the lifeboat as her crew strained their eyes for any sight of the dinghy. Just as hope was almost gone the bowman gave a shout, 'On the starboard bow,' and sure enough a small object could be seen, not very far away. As the boat approached the object sighted resolved itself into two small heads, only a few inches above water. Within minutes the two boys were safely in the lifeboat.

It appears that after drifting for some time their dinghy grounded on a sandbank and, not unnaturally the boys decided that the sand seemed safer than their rather flimsy craft which in any case was taking them further and further from home, so they proceeded to step ashore. Unfortunately the tide was flowing and the dinghy floated away. The water rose steadily and at last it was approaching the younger boy's mouth. His brother then lifted him in his arms, holding his head above water and it was thus that the lifeboat found them. In a very short time the elder boy, too, would have been out of his depth and both would have been drowned.

It is a marvel that two small boys should have kept their heads and not panicked under circumstances which would have tested the nerve of many a brave man. The satisfaction of the lifeboat crew at rescuing two such brave youngsters can well be realised. The coxswain's local knowledge, which allowed him to estimate the direction in which the dinghy would drift, is also to be admired. In every way this was a rescue of which the RNLI was and is justly proud.

Many long and arduous lifeboat services have been undertaken as a result of appeals for assistance to sick and injured persons or to take maternity cases to hospital. Remote islands with little or no medical facilities relied for many years on the lifeboat either to bring a doctor or nurse or take the patient to the nearest hospital. Today such duties are often undertaken by helicopter if one is available and conditions are suitable, but some lifeboat stations still deal with more medical cases than any other type of service.

The remote island of St Kilda once asked for medical assistance to deal with a sick member of the crew of a Spanish trawler who had been landed there. The man was seriously ill and beyond the medical resources of the small community on the island. A helicopter was sent from a Scottish airfield but had to turn back owing to extreme weather conditions and the Barra island, Outer Hebrides, lifeboat was asked to undertake the mission.

This was agreed and the lifeboat proceeded in gale force winds and heavy seas to make the 70 mile passage to the lonely St Kilda.

When they arrived the sick man was placed on board the lifeboat. He was running a high temperature and as the boat made her way back through the stormy seas to Barra island he became delirious and had to be restrained by members of the lifeboat crew who took it in turns to attend to him.

The scene can perhaps be imagined; the crew of the lifeboat, no doubt weary after their long, rough journey to St Kilda, desperately trying to prevent the sick man from injury, in the confined space of the small cabin with the boat plunging wildly in the heavy seas. But this was not all they had to contend with; on their arrival back at Barra, with thoughts no doubt of a hot bath, a hot meal and a warm bed, they were greeted by their local doctor who told them that they must stay in the boat until they had been inoculated as it was now known that the Spanish seaman had typhoid!

Not all rescue work is carried out in heavy weather at sea. Floods and heavy snow on shore have more than once led to calls for lifeboat assistance. These inland missions often lead to some misgivings on the part of those responsible for control of the lifeboats since their main duty is to render assistance to people in trouble at sea and in conditions which call for the particular abilities of these sturdy craft. If a call for assistance should come from a ship while the lifeboat was away on some less arduous mission there could well be criticism as to why she was allowed to go. Nevertheless, expediency must nearly always colour decisions and very rarely have the services of a lifeboat been denied when it is known that people were being subjected to acute discomfort if not in immediate danger.

An incident of this kind occurred during the floods of February 1937 when 12 days of heavy gales and torrential rain caused havoc in Scotland. During this time the Aberdeen lifeboats – there were two stationed there – were very busy and on one occasion spent 22 hours at sea searching for a trawler in a full gale from the south-east. The rivers Dee and

Don had risen rapidly owing to the heavy rain and had overflowed their banks in several places causing extensive flooding to the surrounding countryside. On the morning of 25 January the police telephoned to the lifeboat station saying that Waterside farm, some distance above Bridge of Dee, had been flooded and that a woman and two men were signalling for help from the upper storey of the farmhouse. The gale was still blowing and it was bitterly cold.

The pulling and sailing lifeboat *William and Ellen Robson*, which was on a carriage towed by a tractor, was taken some three miles by road to a point on the river bank above the farm. Here she was launched into the flooded river and carried swiftly by the current soon arrived at the farmhouse. The coxswain manoeuvred the boat close to the building and by means of a ladder the woman, the two men, a cat and a dog were brought down into the boat. The RNLI history of the station records that the coxswain took the lifeboat stern first through the front door of the farmhouse! It must have been a large door. The account goes on to say that the farmhouse is now one of the local points of interest shown to coach tours. With the rescued party on board the lifeboat was rowed back to the place where her carriage was, hauled out of the river and replaced on it and towed back by road to her station. Other reports of services to people marooned by floods includes one in which three men were rescued from a floating haystack and in a number of cases lifeboats have been used to take food to people cut off by water or deep snow.

In not every case in which a lifeboat has been called out to investigate or render assistance has this attention been received with gratitude. On one occasion the Plymouth lifeboat was asked to investigate a report that what appeared to be a body was lying on the beach in Jennycliff bay and on a fine summer night proceeded to carry out this mission. On arrival at the point indicated the boat's searchlight was switched on and soon picked up an object which was obviously the one reported. The lifeboat promptly returned to her station without further action as, the coxswain explained, there was not one body but two, in a sleeping-bag and very much alive. This simple exploit had something in common with an accident to a Canadian rescue hovercraft which returned from a night patrol badly damaged. Her captain reported that in the course of their inspection of the shoreline the searchlight illuminated a female figure about to have what he described as a 'skinny dip'. At this moment, he continued, the hovercraft suddenly developed intense 'rudder judder' with the result that they hit a marking post with some force. The damage was extensive and the repairs expensive.

Some of the old swashbuckling instincts from the time of Drake or before still affect the seafarers of today, particularly on some parts of the coast. At Dover there is, and no doubt always has been, a hardy race of boatmen who make their living with their motor launches by rendering a number of services to other seafarers. One of these consists in putting pilots aboard ships off the harbour and taking pilots off outward bound vessels. Ships indicate that they have a pilot on board who wishes to be landed by hoisting a numeral pendant which also shows which boatman is requested to carry out this duty. On one occasion the Dover lifeboat was out at sea on exercise with the RNLI inspector on board when the coxswain suddenly remarked:

'There's a ship flying my pendant, sir. I didn't expect her until this afternoon. Would you mind if I took the pilot off. I don't want to let him down.'

The inspector quite naturally agreed, the incident adding to the value of the inspection with the necessity of going alongside a large vessel in a seaway. The pilot was soon aboard the lifeboat and insisted that he was quite happy to remain on board for the rest of the exercise and in fact seemed to enjoy the unexpected experience. However, when the lifeboat returned to her berth in the harbour a very irate boatman from another firm was waiting and proceeded to call the coxswain by a lot of very unusual names. It transpired that the pendant the ship was flying was his and not the lifeboat coxswain's who, it seemed, had tried to pull a fast one over a competitor. Whatever the reason for the dispute, the inspector was able to settle the matter before it got to fisticuffs and apparently the right claimant got the fee.

Another coxswain was involved in a rather amusing incident some time afterwards. He was out in his own launch when he heard from the coastguard that a yacht was anchored in an apparently dangerous position close to the Shakespeare cliff, so he proceeded to investigate. On reaching the yacht he found only one man on board, sitting in the cockpit.

Now at that time a notorious criminal was reported to be

on the run from a northern prison and probably heading for the continent. In view of this, the coxswain explained later, he decided to return to Dover and launch the lifeboat with a full crew before taking any further action. This he did and in due course the yacht was towed back to Dover. Here it became clear that the sole occupant was in fact no criminal – on the contrary he was the governor of Dover prison! The odd thing was that the coxswain should have known him well by sight as he was a very keen yachtsman. Whatever the explanation, it never reached the files of the RNLI.

The fact that a wreck was looked upon by local inhabitants as a source of all sorts of unexpected benefits has been mentioned but there are few authentic records of what actually happened at the time, for fairly obvious reasons. One such incident was, however, duly recorded in the journal of the RNLI and this gives some idea of what may have happened in a number of other cases.

In January 1890 the barque *Thorne* went ashore on the rocks off Onchan head in the Isle of Man at half past two in the morning. She had been sheltering in Douglas bay for some days but in the continuing gale conditions her anchor began to drag and eventually she drove ashore. The captain, crew and two passengers were able to get away in one of the ship's boats and were rescued in the nick of time just as they were being driven ashore. The lifeboat which saved them was one of two stationed at Douglas, the *Thomas Rose*.

A fortnight later the *Thorne* went to pieces and, as the accounts of the time describe, the inhabitants of Douglas indulged in an orgy of plunder.

The *Thorne* had been bound from Liverpool to Adelaide with a general cargo which, as the name implies, consisted of everything from tintacks to tricycles. Amongst other things her manifest listed bar iron, grinding stones, silk, crockery, linen, flannel, cured fish and paper. Also included were large quantities of beer, wine and spirits. The report says that the shore was strewn with this sort of debris as well as great quantities of timber.

The customs officers were soon on the spot but they were heavily outnumbered by the mob who were busy hiding away stolen goods in the caves and crevices in the cliffs lining the shore. The customs officers seized a number of barrels of spirits and stowed them in a cave but even when the entrance to this was closed by high water the people clambered down the rocks and secured a cask at the risk of their lives. Having obtained it they stove in the head and were drinking from the cask until the customs men caught them at it and knocked the cask over. Then, the account records with obvious horror, the men scooped up the spirits flowing on the ground, using their seaboots to do it and then could be seen drinking out of their boots!

Apart from the casks, bottles were lying about everywhere and the customs men searched all suspects and removed many bottles from the pockets of plunderers. As might be expected, the drinking of large quantities of neat spirits made many of the men unconscious. There is no mention of women in the report but no doubt some of them felt it their duty to assist their menfolk. It was pointed out that it was bitterly cold and that many of the men would have met their deaths if the police had not collected them in carts and conveyed them to Douglas gaol. Several men had to be taken to hospital where a stomach pump assisted their recovery. As an epilogue we are told that 12 sorry-looking – and no doubt feeling – culprits faced the High Bailiff next day. Elsewhere will be found an entirely different story describing how the coast rescue teams attended the wreck.

Something over a hundred years ago the 'back of the Wight' as the southern side of that island is known, had a reputation for pillaging and generally profiting by other peoples misfortunes. One old inhabitant of the island, when asked what his father did for a living replied 'He just sat around. The sea always brought him something. We lived comfortable enough on that.'

At one time there were lifeboat stations at Ventnor, Atherfield, Brighstone and Brook but all these were closed some time ago. In their day they carried out many fine rescues but with the passing of the square-rigger the need for lifeboats on this stretch of coast grew less and less. The first service of the Brighstone lifeboat was to a vessel called the *Cedarine*. After a mighty struggle against wind and wave the boat, propelled by a dozen men bending their backs to the long oars, fetched up alongside the casualty in time to pluck three men from the sea who had made an early jump for it. One of the rescued men pointed to his two companions and said 'There's another 350 of them on board.'

'Them, what's them?' bellowed the coxswain.

'Convicts,' was the terse answer.

And so there were. Eventually the large collection of malefactors, or most of them, reached the shore and dispersing with military precision amongst the surrounding villages proceeded to institute a night of terror for the inhabitants. It was the biggest gaol break on record, or very nearly so.

With a view to making the most of their unexpected freedom and perhaps to celebrate their escape from what might have been an unpleasant conclusion to their sentences, the convicts first provided unwanted custom for all the inns they could find. No doubt they managed to deplete the stocks rapidly and probably asked for the score to be put on the slate. In their favour it must be said that according to reports they did not attempt to molest people in their homes and merely moved further inland as they drank inn after inn dry.

As soon as the facts were known steps were put in hand to round up the roysterers and troops were employed for what must have been a rather unpleasant task, for having drink taken the convicts soon quarrelled amongst themselves and pitched battles took place all over the island. It was days before the last of these unwelcome survivors was rounded up and one cannot help feeling that some at least must have taken advantage of the opportunity to fade away quietly into the background and start a new life in another guise.

A strange but rather grim incident in which the Southend-on-Sea lifeboat was involved arose as a result of a fire in a Dutch ship, the motor vessel *Temar*, in December 1962. The coastguard had reported the ship on fire near No. 2 sea reach buoy and the Southend lifeboat *Greater London II* (Civil Service No. 30) launched at 1330. Two tugs, a local boat and the tanker *Mobil Enterprise* were already standing by the casualty whose master said he did not need lifeboat assistance. Coxswain Gilson nevertheless decided to proceed as he feared lives might be in danger. The weather was overcast with a fresh to strong south-west wind.

As the lifeboat circled the *Temar* the coxswain saw a man's head sticking out of a porthole on the starboard quarter. He was apparently unable to get out of the cabin he was in and was having difficulty in breathing owing to smoke and fumes. The *Mobil Enterprise* had already put on board her chief engineer, second officer and a deck hand with an asbestos suit and breathing apparatus but they were unable to reach the man's head.

By this time the wind had increased to gale force and the

flames were rapidly approaching the cabin in which the man was trapped. A tug had now got a line on the *Temar* and towed her round to make a lee for the lifeboat which made fast alongside the trapped man's porthole with the crew tending warps to keep her in position. Two lifeboatmen boarded the casualty and by lying flat on the deck were able to hold the man's head out of the porthole 'by hanging on to his ears' as they described it. As the lifeboat rose on a wave the coxswain and mechanic clapped the mask on the man's face and gave him a whiff of oxygen. This they were only able to do for a few seconds at a time owing to the motion of the lifeboat but it kept the victim from losing consciousness.

Even so, it became clear that the flames were getting closer and that more drastic action was required so oxy-acetylene cutting equipment was brought from the tug. As the deck above him was being cut away a hose was played on the trapped man as molten metal was falling on his back. As soon as the opening in the deck had been made large enough the chief engineer of the *Mobil Enterprise*, dressed in an asbestos suit, was able to extricate the survivor who was put on board the lifeboat and landed at Southend pier where a doctor and an ambulance were waiting. On the way ashore the man's burns were treated by the bowman of the lifeboat and on arrival at the pier the doctor administered morphia before allowing him to be lifted ashore. This service is considered to be one of the most unusual ever recorded.

Chapter 8

Rescue by helicopter and by breeches buoy

The development of the helicopter during and immediately after World War II provided a new and exciting means of rescue. The ability of the helicopter to hover, even in high winds, and the winch gear which allowed a rescued person to be hauled up to the machine, meant that people could be snatched from dangerous positions which probably could not be approached by any other method. The earlier helicopters could not operate in very high winds or at night, so that their operational use was restricted. Today, these limitations have been largely if not completely overcome, as have other drawbacks such as their comparatively short radius of action and small carrying capacity.

The rescue helicopter's main function originally was to render assistance to aircraft which had come down in the sea. In fact this type of casualty fortunately has been rare and the rescue of swimmers and people from all sorts of surface craft has provided the bulk of the work for this branch of the rescue service.

Naturally the advent of the helicopter produced a good deal of discussion on the subject of sea rescue and a number of otherwise knowledgeable people suggested that it had rendered the lifeboat obsolete. Certainly the helicopter carried out quickly and effectively a number of rescues which at one time would have fallen to a lifeboat to perform. Indeed, for a time there was intense rivalry between the lifeboat and the helicopter, at least on the part of the lifeboat crews who were naturally despondent when beaten to a casualty by the much faster helicopter.

An incident of this kind in which the lifeboatmen were not so upset occurred at Eastbourne a number of years ago. Telling the story, the coxswain explained that they got a call to launch to the assistance of a man and a boy cut off by the tide at the foot of Beachy Head. 'But,' he declared, 'we wiped the eyes of the helicopter boys this time.'

It appears that it was low water when the call came and at Eastbourne this can mean a very difficult launch. In spite of this the lifeboat got away smartly and she was halfway to Beachy when a helicopter came in sight and quickly lifted first one body then another from the beach and deposited them on the cliff top. At this point it was suggested to the coxswain that the lifeboat seemed to have come off second best again. He shook his head with a grin and said that there was more to tell.

He explained that the man and the boy were father and son and when they were set down on the cliff top there were all sorts of people waiting to help them; coastguards, ambulance men, police and RWVS ladies with hot drinks. When asked to make his choice of the services available the man said:

'Please, I would like to be put back on the beach again. I have been collecting driftwood down there for twenty years and if I ever get cut off by the tide I shall deserve it. Or, if you prefer it, you can bring my pile of driftwood up here.'

'So you see we did come off best that time, after all,' insisted the coxswain; and perhaps he was right.

Another story is told of a similar misunderstanding and this incident happened on the Cornish coast. It was reported that a bather had entered the water and swum immediately out to sea and as far as could be seen he was still swimming strongly in that direction. The coastguard requested the assistance of a helicopter and within minutes a machine was hovering over the swimmer. The man refused to get into the strop that was lowered to him so the pilot decided to use a scoop which was carried at that time. This was attached to the winch wire and the pilot skilfully netted the swimmer as if he had been a big fish. Very shortly afterwards he landed his catch.

On shore the rescued man showed no signs of gratitude at all and in fact protested strongly at the treatment he had received. It appeared that he had been practising for a cross-channel swim and was in no danger at all. To make matters worse his clothes were on the other side of the bay and could they get them, please?

Such amusing incidents add a touch of cheerful humour to what can be an extremely difficult and dangerous job.

Everything depends on the skill of the pilot and his crew and split second decisions frequently have to be made. Should the winch wire become fast or entangled in quite a small craft it must be cut at once or the helicopter would almost certainly crash. This has happened more than once and even, regrettably, during an exercise with a lifeboat, the crew of which expressed some satisfaction at rescuing a helicopter crew.

Possibly one of the most important functions of the helicopter arises from its ability to provide rapid medical assistance to sick and injured people on board ship, sometimes many miles from the shore. Not only on board ship of course but on outlying islands and remote or otherwise inaccessible places on the mainland. Indeed, there must be many people alive today who would have died had it not been for the versatility of the helicopter and the skill and bravery of the pilots and crews.

It is always difficult to select outstanding rescues from the many fine examples, particularly as it is not always the most obvious ones which called for the greatest skill and courage. Sometimes a very clever and courageous effort goes almost unnoticed and unrewarded, just as in wartime many gallant deeds fail to win the medal they deserved.

It is perhaps not surprising that one of the earliest and most unexpected rescues by helicopter was carried out by an American pilot flying from Manston airfield in Kent. The story began in November 1954 when a series of strong gales persisted over a number of days causing ships to seek shelter all round the coast. On 27 November the South Goodwin lightvessel reported that her anchor was dragging and she began to drift.

The Ramsgate lifeboat launched immediately as the Walmer crew had to remove a large bank of shingle built up by the gales, before they could launch their boat. As the position of the lightship was now in some doubt the coastguard also suggested that the Dover lifeboat should join the search. The Dover lifeboat is moored in what was a wartime bombproof shelter known as 'The Pens' and on the night in question the crew had some difficulty in getting along the harbour wall owing to flying debris scattered by the gale. After a struggle they managed to board the boat and were soon meeting the heavy seas as they passed through the eastern entrance to the harbour.

All night the search went on as the lifeboats plunged along

the edge of the Goodwin sands in the heavy breaking seas for which the area is notorious. At daybreak they were informed that the lightship had been located and soon she was sighted, lying on her beam ends on the sands against which she had for so long acted as a warning to shipping. The tide had ebbed since the lightship went aground and the lifeboats found that there was not sufficient water to get nearer than 150 yards (135 metres).

To the astonishment of the lifeboat crews, at this moment a helicopter appeared and at the same time a survivor could be seen, moving with difficulty on the casualty owing to the acute angle of the deck. Having made apparently a preliminary survey of the situation the helicopter quickly winched up the survivor and proceeded back to Manston with him.

The survivor, by some strange chance, was not a member of the crew of the lightship but a bird watcher, carrying out observations for the Ministry of Agriculture and Fisheries. He was Donald Murton and he was 22 years of age. The seven members of the lightship's crew were all drowned. This sudden and shattering disaster served to emphasise the devotion to duty of the Trinity House crews and the very real dangers they face in the course of their normally unspectacular work.

The pilot of the helicopter was Captain Curtis E. Parkins of the United States Air Force and for this very efficient rescue he was subsequently awarded the silver medal of the RNLI, thus becoming the first pilot of an aircraft to receive one of the Institution's medals.

Probably the most ambitious and spectacular helicopter rescues up to the present time took place in February 1953 when the Norwegian ship *Dovrefjell* went ashore on the Pentland skerries at the eastern end of the notorious Pentland firth, one of the most turbulent stretches of water in the world. The Pentland firth has a deservedly sinister reputation with seamen and indeed with any travellers who have had the misfortune to meet it at its worst. Currents of up to nine knots give the islands in the firth the appearance of steaming at high speed, leaving a long widening wake of white water.

The vessel's master reported the mishap by wireless saying that the ship was in no danger. She was bound from Newcastle-on-Tyne to Canada in ballast and had a crew of 41 which included 31 Italians. Her messages were received and re-transmitted by Wick radio and as a result the coastguard passed the information to Longhope lifeboat station in the Orkney islands. Soon after five o'clock in the morning the lifeboat *Thomas McCunn* was launched and shortly afterwards the Wick lifeboat *City of Edinburgh* proceeded.

The Wick lifeboat reached the *Dovrefjell* first and found her fast on a rocky ledge on the south side of Little Skerry. The high, confused seas were breaking over her in the strong southerly wind and ebb tide and her master told the lifeboat coxswain that it would be impossible for him to get alongside under those conditions. About eight o'clock the Longhope lifeboat arrived but in the meantime the captain of a naval vessel in the vicinity had been in touch with the naval air station at Lossiemouth and two naval helicopters arrived. These soon started picking up members of the crew of the casualty and landing them on the mainland. As one helicopter winched up a man from the bridge of the ship where her crew had sought shelter, the other waited its turn and then carried out the same procedure. In this way 31 men were rescued and landed at John O'Groats.

During the whole of this operation the two lifeboats stood by, ready to render assistance either to the ship or the helicopters. Later in the morning another helicopter arrived from the RAF station at Leuchars.

The master and nine men decided to remain on board but eventually changed their minds and were taken ashore by the RAF helicopter at midday. This was an extremely well organised and efficiently executed operation in far from easy conditions in what was the comparatively early days of the helicopter and gave a good idea of the scope of this method of rescue. The small helicopters in service at that time had quite short endurance in the air and were unable to fly the direct course from Lossiemouth which would have been almost entirely over the sea, so it was necessary to make fairly extensive refuelling arrangements.

The Longhope and Wick lifeboats returned to their stations after what was a useful but unrewarding duty – not an unusual situation for lifeboat crews. However, their efforts were recognised by the Norwegian government, the King of Norway also awarding medals to Coxswain Kirkpatrick of Longhope and Coxswain Stewart of Wick. Expressions of thanks were also received from the Italian government.

Almost certainly one of the most dramatic and dangerous rescues by helicopter and breeches buoy took place against the rock bound cliffs of Land's End. In November 1962 the coastguard on watch at Cape Cornwall observed the lights of a trawler proceeding south through the channel between the Longships reef and the mainland. It was five o'clock in the morning and a strong northerly wind was blowing with heavy rain squalls. As he watched, the fishing vessel altered course towards the land and almost at once a red distress rocket burst in the sky. The rescue services were quickly alerted. The Sennen cove lifeboat launched at 0521 and the coast rescue teams with their line-throwing gear made their way along the cliffs from Sennen and St Just. A helicopter at the RAF station Chivenor stood by.

The casualty proved to be the *Jeanne Gougy* of Dieppe and she had gone ashore on the north side of Land's End. Here she was found, rolling and grinding on the rocks in the heavy swell which broke over her in great sheets of foam. How she got there was and remains a mystery for the skipper and anyone who might have provided the answer was washed overboard and drowned, probably almost as soon as the vessel struck.

The coastguard teams on the cliff could hear cries from the crew of the trawler below them and in the light of a parachute flare could make out five or six men in the wing of the bridge. Six rocket lines were fired over the casualty, three of them actually falling across her wheelhouse but they fouled the rigging and could not be reached by the survivors. One of the men made a gallant effort to secure one of the lines but was swept overboard to his death. Next moment an angry sea ripped away the wheelhouse doors and the water poured in in a torrent. Another wave completed the destruction, turning the trawler right over on her side and washing the rest of the sheltering men away to their doom.

The Sennen lifeboat, when she arrived on the scene was unable to close the trawler which now lay on the rocks – high, but certainly not dry as huge waves swept in and over her. It seemed certain that nobody could possibly be alive on board and there were no signs of movement but the lifeboat recovered two bodies from the surf. The helicopter from Chivenor also arrived and found another body and both continued to search but without success. Eventually, as it appeared that nothing more could be done the lifeboat set course for Newlyn to land the bodies and the helicopter returned to refuel. The District Officer of Coastguard, Mr J. C. Bridger and his crew remained on watch in order to search the trawler when the tide had ebbed sufficiently to allow them to go on board.

Suddenly there was a shout. 'There's somebody alive on board!'

A lady amongst those watching had seen an arm waving from inside the remains of the wheelhouse and a man was heard to call out. As the vessel had been nearly submerged in angry seas for almost six hours this seemed incredible but there was no doubt about it. The coastguard cautioned the man to stay where he was and as further waves broke over the ship the onlookers were afraid that he too had been washed away.

More rockets were fired and again a line dropped over the wheelhouse but it was beyond the man's reach. By manoeuvring the line from the cliff top the rescue team managed to get it near enough for the man to seize. After some difficulty he was able to make it fast and the breeches buoy was sent across. By now the helicopter had returned and as it hovered over the casualty one after another four men emerged from inside the trawler and were safely hauled to the cliff top in the breeches buoy.

But the drama was not over for the excited onlookers. The helicopter lowered Flight Sergeant Eric Smith on to the wreck and he promptly hauled an exhausted man out of the battered wheelhouse and was winched up with him into the helicopter. Then he returned to the trawler again and this time rescued a boy in the same way, after which he made a search of the vessel and confirmed that there was now no hope of any other members of the crew being left alive on board. Thus six men were rescued by the determined efforts of the coastguard teams with their rocket apparatus and by the RAF helicopter, flying in dangerous proximity to the steep cliffs of Land's End. The lifeboat had to be content with the melancholy task of retrieving and landing the bodies of drowned men. Yet its immediate reply to the call to launch and presence at the scene of rescue added an additional safety measure even though lack of sufficient depth of water made it impossible for the boat to get near enough to save lives.

Another fine rescue by the coastguard took place at Hartland point in Devon in the same month. The incident began when the Royal Fleet Auxiliary *Green Ranger*, a tanker of 3,500 tons, drove ashore in a severe gale and high seas. She had been under tow from Plymouth to Cardiff but the tug *Caswell* had been forced to slip the towrope when she was hit by a huge wave. The *Green Ranger* was then at the mercy of the wind and sea and drifted rapidly towards the shore, grounding stern first on the rocks at the bottom of a 400 feet high cliff in the pitch darkness. The seven men who formed her crew for the tow made their way to the highest point of the ship and huddled there in the dark, listening to the creaking and groaning of the steel plates as the ship pounded on the rocks. It may well have seemed to them that the chances of rescue, either from sea or land, were very slim indeed.

But the alarm had been given and the rescue services moved swiftly into action. The Clovelly and Appledore lifeboats launched in appalling conditions and the Coast Rescue team under the District Officer of Coastguard, George Read, made their way to the scene but not without some difficulty. The Clovelly lifeboat, one of the 35ft 6in Liverpool type, made very little progress in the very heavy seas off Hartland, filling with water and generally giving her crew a wet and uncomfortable time and a certain amount of apprehension. Eventually she was forced to return to Clovelly. Her radio was now out of action and the shore helpers burnt flares to warn her that landing was dangerous as the seas were breaking over the harbour wall and the beach was considered impossible. The entrance was attempted nevertheless and a big sea nearly brought disaster. Fortunately this was followed by a lull and the boat was brought ashore without further damage.

The Appledore lifeboat was experiencing just the same conditions but as a larger craft she was standing up to the pounding somewhat better. The Hartland Coast Rescue crew were valiantly dragging the rocket and breeches buoy gear across the fields on the cliffs above with the aid of a tractor. It was quite dark when they got into position and the wind estimated at force 10 with frequent hail showers. A searchlight was brought into action and in its beam two rockets were fired towards the *Green Ranger* but both fell short. It was then decided that it would be impossible to reach the casualty from the cliff top and it would be necessary to wait until the gear could be rigged at the bottom of the cliff.

Three men made the risky journey in the dark down to the foot of the cliff to determine whether it would be possible to get the gear, some of it very heavy, down to the beach. It was decided to try and the work commenced.

During this time the Appledore boat had reached the casualty which was found to be still lying stern on to the rocks. Coxswain Sidney Cann took the lifeboat in so close that it seemed almost possible to step on the rocks surrounding them. From this distance there was no sign of any survivors and repeated calls on the loud-hailer failed to produce any reply. The position of the lifeboat was far too dangerous for dallying close at hand so Cann took the boat off shore and stood by in case there was any possibility of finding survivors. In fact, the crew of the *Green Ranger* were still huddled in what shelter they could find and afterwards one man said he saw the lifeboat approaching but the others did not believe him. Conditions were so terrible that no-one expected a rescue attempt from seawards.

The coastguard team had managed to get their gear down the cliff and across the slippery rocks to a position near enough to the tanker to reach her with a rocket. They fired and the first shot went right across the ship and dropped the line over her. But the men on board had heard nothing because of the roar of the sea and had no idea that rescue was at hand. Just as the second rocket was about to be fired the survivors realised that a line had reached them and in a few minutes they had hauled the warp on board and made the tail block fast. Out came the breeches buoy and one by one the exhausted men were pulled to safety. It was indeed a classic breeches buoy rescue and one of which HM Coastguard have every reason to be proud.

January 1974 produced a series of heavy gales which took a grievous toll of coastal shipping. On 16 January the 800-ton Danish coaster *Merc Enterprise* was labouring in heavy seas off the south Devon coast when she developed a list, either from cargo shifting or from the water she had taken on board. At 1345 the captain, Jan Fedderson, realised that his ship was lower in the water and wallowing sluggishly. He sent out a distress signal asking for immediate assistance.

All the rescue services were alerted and a Russian trawler in the vicinity altered course and put on full speed for the position given by the *Merc Enterprise*. Shortly afterwards a huge wave broke over the sinking vessel which took on a critical list. The captain gave orders to abandon ship. There were 19 people on board including the captain's wife and the chief engineer's fiancée; all had already donned their life-jackets.

Just as the Russian trawler *Leningrad* arrived the *Merc Enterprise* capsized and those on board were soon struggling in the sea. Some had already abandoned ship. The Russians managed to rescue four people just as four *Sea King* helicopters arrived from the naval air station at Culdrose. Two of these were manned by German air force crews training in Britain.

Conditions were appalling with high breaking seas and a gale force wind. In addition the survivors were too exhausted to get themselves into the harness lowered to them and helicopter crew members had to descend with double harness to assist them and get them back into the aircraft. The 15-year-old deck boy of the ship kept himself afloat for three-quarters of an hour before being picked up. The helicopters saved seven people in all, making 11 survivors with those picked up by the Russian trawler. Six men and the captain's wife were lost.

As a result of this dramatic and determined helicopter rescue five naval fliers from Culdrose received medals for gallantry. Two of the helicopters had to make forced landings in the dark on returning from the mission owing to engine failure, probably due to the continuous exposure to salt spray. The fact that the pilots were able to accomplish such difficult emergency landings in the dark and after a long period of intense concentration, pays great tribute to their skill and endurance.

Almost exactly a year later another drama of the sea was played out off the Cornish coast in very similar conditions. This time it was the British ship *Lovat* of 1,093 tons, on passage from Swansea to France with a cargo of anthracite dust, that became a casualty. Having delayed her sailing from Swansea for three days because of bad weather the unfortunate vessel met winds of from gale to storm force off Land's End. In mountainous seas her cargo shifted giving the ship a dangerous list. Her master sent out a distress call at 0600 and the Penlee lifeboat launched. Ships in the vicinity altered course for the position and at first light a Whirlwind helicopter took off from Culdrose. Aboard the Whirlwind, which is a small machine, was Leading Aircrewman Peter Gibbs who had only finished his training as a search and rescue diver the week previously. His story is perhaps best told in his own words:

'When we got there at about 0800 the ship had already sunk. There were rescue ships about but the waves were 20 feet high and it was too rough for them to get alongside the rafts and take the survivors off. There were six of them there but when I was winched down I found that two were already dead, probably from exposure. I helped a survivor into the harness and signalled "go" to the winch operator. Just then a big wave washed over the raft and the chopper lost sight of us. There was a huge loop in the winchwire which would have sliced through my arm if it had tightened so the operator had to cut the wire at the winch. The two of us fell into the sea but we managed to swim back to the raft which was awash. The tops of the waves were breaking right across us. Two of the men looked desperate. I tried to keep one young fellow alive but he was too far gone and he died in my arms. It must have been from exposure. The fourth fellow died too.

'After what seemed a long time two Sea King helicopters (a much larger type) arrived and I knew they would be able to handle it. I got two survivors winched up and then three of the bodies but they were so heavy and took so much time that we had to leave the fourth body as the survivors were badly in need of treatment.'

Once more the lifeboat had the melancholy task of recovering and landing five bodies at Newlyn. Other bodies were picked up by HMS *Wilton*.

According to the survivors they all mustered in the wheelhouse when it seemed probable that the *Lovat* would capsize. Then the captain decided that the time had come to abandon ship so a liferaft was launched and worked round to the stern. All hands made their way aft and endeavoured to jump into the raft but some landed in the sea and were hauled aboard by their shipmates. Owing to the heavy list it was impossible to launch either of the ship's lifeboats or the other liferaft. There was soon about two feet of water in the liferaft and as some of the men had not had time to don warm clothing the effects of exposure on a cold winter day were soon felt.

It was stated that anthracite dust was considered a safe cargo but the fact that in this case it apparently shifted would seem to indicate that at least some precautions are necessary.

It is good to know that the splendid efforts and extreme bravery of Leading Aircrewman Peter Gibbs were subsequently recognised by the award of the Queen's Gallantry Medal, which even from the bare details given here was well and truly earned.

There is one rather pleasant little story which sums up the relationship between lifeboats and helicopters rather neatly. One of the lifeboats on the north-east coast – it might be wise not to be more precise – had been out on service and owing to the weather conditions was unable to rehouse at her own station. In order to ride out the storm the coxswain anchored the boat in the lee of an island and there he and his crew just had to await a change in the weather. But alas this was slow in coming and after a number of hours, having consumed all the provisions that a lifeboat carries and being cold and wet the lifeboatmen began to lose some of their habitual stoicism. They began to debate ways and means of alleviating their plight and somebody suggested, probably as a joke, that they should ask for helicopter assistance. But the idea met with immediate general approval so the radio telephone was used to suggest that the local air station might like to oblige with a little taxi service.

No sooner asked than complied with! A helicopter appeared, lifted the somewhat surprised crew into the air and conveyed them to within handy distance of their homes. When the lifeboatmen had had a change of clothes and a hot meal the helicopter swiftly lifted them again and lowered them gently into their boat with expressions of goodwill. One can almost hear the air crew saying, 'Any time, chaps. Any time.' It is not known what the old stagers of that part of the coast thought about all this but one can guess that there was a good deal of not entirely sympathetic comment in the various public houses.

The work of the coastguard Coast Rescue service although frequently unspectacular may well involve great hardship and determination, not only in the actual work of rescue but often in just getting to a spot near enough to a wreck for the rockets to reach it. In a number of incidents there has been a considerable element of danger for some of the men in the team but they are rarely greeted as heroes.

A very early case in which the difficulties of the rescue

teams did attract attention occurred when the barque *Thorne* went ashore in the Isle of Man, as is mentioned elsewhere. On this occasion the Rocket Brigade as it was then called had, as the RNLI journal described it ' – a terrible time getting to the spot. There was no roadway from below Derby Castle in those days and the brigade had to go up Burnt Mill hill and along the brow above Port-e-Vada.' They were then held up by a stile and had to unload their cart and manhandle all their gear before setting out across the fields towards Onchan harbour. The fields were beset with every conceivable hazard in the shape of swamps, briars and barbed-wire fences interspersed with newly ploughed soil. Through these obstructions they were guided by the miserable light of hand lamps, some of which blew out and could not be relit because of the gale and the lashing rain which well soaked everybody. It was pitch dark and part of their route lay along the edge of the cliff on a narrow path with a fatal drop on one side. In this 'awkward business' as the account put it they were assisted by the police. Since these manful efforts in the end proved abortive it would not be surprising to learn that there were few cheerful faces when the Rocket Brigade finally returned to their homes.

Chapter 9

Services to yachts & aircraft

Every year the calls for assistance from craft round the coast of Britain increase steadily in number. In the last 20 years or so the work of the sea rescue services has changed in character quite considerably. Now by far the greater percentage of casualties is made up of pleasure craft, from tiny inflatable dinghies to large motor cruisers. Everyone seems to want to get afloat and this includes swimmers, anglers and indeed divers, although these last spend more time under rather than on the water. But a number of divers have been rescued for they are not entirely immune from the dangers of drowning.

For a variety of reasons, services to yachts are not usually attended with the same amount of danger for the lifeboatmen as those to larger vessels but this does not mean that they are not often arduous and difficult as this first example shows. On the Sussex coast on the morning of Sunday 8 August 1948 a strong gale was blowing with a very rough sea and swell. Soon after 0830 the Shoreham coastguard sighted a yacht about three miles off shore, driving along the coast before the gale, her sails torn and she appeared to be out of control. He rang the lifeboat station and at 0915 the lifeboat *Rosa Woodd and Phyllis Lunn* went sliding down the slipway. She had a rough passage across the harbour bar in heavy, breaking seas and then, hoisting her auxiliary sails to assist her engine, she settled down to a long, hard chase, for the yacht had a handsome start.

The chase continued for 14 miles until the yacht neared Newhaven, which it seemed she was going to try and enter. The wind had now backed to the southward and was blowing right on shore. As the yacht, the *Gull*, reached the western arm of Newhaven harbour she was about five hundred yards to seaward of it and the pursuing lifeboat was now only a hundred yards astern of her. The yacht made a desperate attempt to fetch the entrance to the harbour but this meant she had to gybe, bringing her mainsail or what was left of it over on to the other tack, a rather hair-raising operation in a gale and broken water. As she gybed, a big sea washed right over her, filling the cockpit and leaving her little more than a waterlogged wreck. She drifted past the harbour entrance and the east pier into the shallow broken water on the other side where she managed to let go an anchor. But the cable parted under the strain and it was clear that nothing could now save the yacht from drifting ashore. On board were three men, two women and a boy.

Driven into the bay by the gale the seas were terrifying and the coxswain of the lifeboat knew how shallow the water was and that if his craft struck the bottom the result might be disastrous. There was no time to weigh up the risks and Coxswain Upperton did not hesitate but steered straight for the casualty. Another sea smothered the lifeboat and when it had cleared the coxswain anxiously counted his crew for he felt sure some must have been washed overboard. But all were still with him and a moment later they were alongside the *Gull* and the survivors were seized without ceremony and dragged into the lifeboat. One man was still aboard the yacht and this meant going in again with even less time to spare but he was quickly plucked from the flooded deck and stowed away in the lifeboat. Upperton wasted not another second and soon had the lifeboat punching her way out of the shallows into deeper water in great sheets of spray. Soon the lifeboat and the survivors were entering the comparative calm of Newhaven harbour.

Many people were watching from the shore and all were agreed that it was a marvellous rescue and not a moment too soon. One onlooker, watching the whole operation through powerful binoculars, described it as a 'Pretty piece of work in severe conditions and very little water.' It is pleasant to be able to record that the owner of the yacht made gifts of £25 to the crew of the lifeboat and £25 to the funds of the RNLI '– as a small tribute to the services rendered by the Institution and to the skill and courage of the lifeboat crew.' The RNLI awarded Coxswain James Upperton a bar to his silver medal and the Thanks on Vellum to the other members of the crew.

The busiest day in the history of the lifeboat service

occurred on 29 July 1956 when a shallow depression in the Atlantic suddenly deepened and came flying along the south coast of Britain with wind speeds of up to 88 knots. Not surprisingly, a lot of very competent seamen were caught out by this unexpected hurricane and along the whole length of the English channel yachts were in trouble. Not only yachts; but the events of this incredible day give a detailed and compact description of the sort of protection that yachtsmen in general receive from the RNLI and the lifeboat crews. In fact, during that 24 hours, 38 lifeboat stations received urgent calls for help and 52 launches on service were made. Fourteen vessels were salved and 107 lives saved. Twelve people were landed and seven vessels assisted. A number of lifeboats were called out three or four times. Medals were awarded for services carried out by the Selsey, Dover and Dungeness lifeboats and by a Whitstable fishing boat. It says much for the efficiency of the lifeboat service and the resolute ability of the crews, that such an unprecedented demand should have been met so calmly and successfully.

29 July 1956 was a Sunday, and just before noon the Selsey coastguard informed the honorary secretary of the Selsey lifeboat station that a small yacht heading towards West Wittering was flying distress signals. At this time there was a strong gale from the south-west.

The Selsey crew had some difficulty in reaching the boathouse, which was some distance from the shore and reached by a long gangway. The wind was so strong that at times it forced the men to go on their hands and knees and the boathouse doors nearly took charge.

The lifeboat *Canadian Pacific* launched down the slipway at 10 minutes past 12, less than quarter of an hour after the call. The sea was a mass of white water and flying spray and it was reported that visitors at a nearby holiday camp who were watching, dropped on their knees to pray for the safety of the crew when they saw the conditions they must face. Almost as soon as the boat hit the water her propellers were fouled by lobster pot lines, the pots having been washed from their usually secure moorings by the force of the gale. Engine revolutions dropped but it was impossible to stop and try and clear the propellers under those conditions and Coxswain Grant had no option but to make his way round Selsey bill at slow speed and hope for the best.

At half past twelve the *Maaslust*, a Dutch boeier yacht of 40 tons was sighted. She was under engine with her sails blown away and was yawing about wildly. She was right in amongst the rocks over which the sea was breaking into great sheets of spray making it difficult to see anything. The coxswain brought the lifeboat up on the port side of the yacht with his bow just forward of her leeboard, which was a major obstacle for coming alongside. Just at that moment a big sea hit the yacht and the lifeboat, sweeping them a long way apart. Just then another yacht was sighted to windward and she seemed to be in more immediate trouble than the *Maaslust*, so Grant decided to take her crew off first.

This was the *Bloodhound*, later to become a Royal yacht, but at this moment she was lying to an anchor with all her sails blown away and a tangle of rigging over her side. She was washing down heavily and all her crew were on deck. She was lying head to wind with the sea on her port side, just to windward of some rocks. Coxswain Grant, who still had only very much reduced engine power, brought the lifeboat up on the yacht's starboard side, nearly bow on, with both the lifeboat and the yacht taking heavy water overall. Lifeboatmen stationed on the fore-deck helped the two women and seven men safely into the lifeboat which wasted no time in going astern out of it. This manoeuvre had an unexpectedly beneficial effect in that it partially cleared some of the lines fouling the propellers and the engine revolutions increased somewhat.

The survivors from the *Bloodhound* were made as comfortable as possible and the lifeboat returned to the *Maaslust* which had not drifted very far. This time Grant decided that he must come up on the weather side and once more the leeboard presented a problem. He therefore drove the lifeboat straight at the low bulwark of the yacht and held her there, bows-on with the engines. There were six people aboard the yacht, three men, a woman and two children, the younger being a baby. They were all wearing lifebelts with lifelines attached and the Selsey crew had some difficulty in clearing these from the rigging. As Coxswain Grant said with a grin afterwards 'The lady nearly screamed her head off when I whipped out my big knife to cut the baby's lifeline which was made fast in the yacht. She thought I was going to cut the baby's throat!'

At the time it was not so funny. In the course of the operation the stem and fendering of the lifeboat were damaged and it was found that the wheel had jammed. Grant gave the order to prepare to anchor as it seemed certain that the lifeboat would drive ashore herself. Just as the order to let go the anchor was about to be given the wheel freed, something having fouled the rudder and apparently cleared as the boat moved.

Coxswain Grant decided to make for Portsmouth with the survivors as it would not have been possible to rehouse at Selsey with such a sea running. They had not gone far when yet another yacht was sighted, nearly on her beam ends. This was the six-metre yacht *Coima* and she was lying to a sea anchor. She had driven across from an anchorage in St Helen's roads and was on the point of going ashore. Grant brought the lifeboat up on her starboard quarter and her crew of three quickly scrambled aboard the lifeboat. But only just in time; *Coima* was full of water and sank almost immediately. Once more, going astern had a beneficial effect on the engine revolutions as more lines and floats were spewed out of the propeller tunnels of the lifeboat.

The time was now 1340, just an hour and a half from the time the *Canadian Pacific* launched but a great deal had happened in that time. At 1645 they reached Portsmouth where the 18 survivors were landed. Food and dry clothing for the crew were provided by the dockyard and the lifeboat left for her station at 1845. On the return another yacht was sighted and the lifeboat made for her but she declined assistance. The *Canadian Pacific* finally reached her moorings at 10 o'clock that night.

Next day it was discovered that the *Bloodhound* was still afloat and it was thought that although she had lost her anchor, the chain had jammed in the rocks and kept her from going ashore. The Selsey lifeboat went off and picked her up and towed her to Portsmouth. For these services the silver medal for gallantry was awarded to Coxswain Douglas Grant and the Thanks on Vellum to the other seven members of his crew.

Further up channel the Dover lifeboat *Southern Africa* was also dealing busily with calls for assistance to yachts. At 1030 on the morning of 29 July the Sandgate coastguard rang up to say that the South Goodwin light-vessel had reported a yacht in difficulties two miles from the entrance to Dover harbour. There was a very rough sea and a strong south-southwesterly gale. It was low water. The lifeboat put to sea immediately and came up with the yacht *Straight Flush* in the reported position. She had a crew of four and with torn sails she was making heavy weather of it. A line was put aboard her and she was towed to Dover.

The lifeboat reached her station again just after noon but was soon called out again as a number of yachts sheltering in the harbour had begun to drag their anchors. The wind had now reached hurricane force with gusts up to 80 knots and there was a steep, confused sea in the harbour. It was half flood when the *Southern Africa* left her moorings again and Coxswain John Walker decided to go to the assistance of the yacht *Mermaid* which had driven close to the Castle jetty but by the time the lifeboat rounded the west pier he found it was too late. The yacht had struck the jetty and broke up in a few minutes, the crew being rescued by ropes thrown from the jetty.

The lifeboat then made for another yacht, the *Tawi*, which was just west of the Castle jetty and in danger of going ashore there or on the rocks to the eastward. The *Tawi* had two anchors down and was yawing wildly in the confused sea. A large motor launch was endeavouring to take her in tow but gave up the attempt when the lifeboat arrived and sought shelter herself. Coxswain Walker had some difficulty in getting alongside the yacht because she was sheering about unpredictably but eventually he managed to get a line with a grapnel fast. The *Tawi*'s crew of three were exhausted and could do little more than hang on to the rigging for dear life.

The *Tawi* was now a bare fifty yards from the shore and about the same distance from the Castle jetty but Walker managed to keep the lifeboat alongside long enough for the survivors to be pulled into safety. A number of the guardrail stanchions of the *Southern Africa* were lost or damaged in the process. The *Tawi* later dragged ashore and became a total loss.

The owner of the yacht *Sonia* which had also come to an anchor but was close inshore and only holding her own by going ahead on her engine, decided he would be better out of it and asked for a tow. Coxswain Walker sized up the situation and decided that it would be too risky to try and get a tow-rope aboard her in that position. He also felt it was necessary to land the crew of the *Tawi* who were obviously in need of some attention. When the lifeboat returned the *Sonia* was flying a distress signal and had dragged further inshore. Once again Walker had some difficulty in getting alongside but finally managed to do so and the yacht's crew were taken off.

The lifeboat then went to the assistance of a third yacht, the *Madame Pompadour*, a 45ft cabin cruiser with a diesel engine. She had two anchors down and her engine going full ahead. She, too, was yawing wildly and rolling heavily. The owner and his son were on board and asked to be taken off. This proved to be anything but easy and it was only after six attempts that the lifeboat got alongside. The owner was a heavy man and transferring him from the plunging yacht to the lifeboat was only achieved with some difficulty. His legs were nearly crushed between the two craft and everyone breathed a sight of relief when the owner and his son were safely on board the *Southern Africa*. Ten minutes later the *Madame Pompadour* broke up on the rocks by the west pier. The seven survivors still on board the lifeboat were landed at the Custom House jetty and the boat returned to her moorings.

For these services a second service clasp to his bronze medal was awarded to Coxswain John Walker and a letter of appreciation was sent to Mr Douglas Stewart, the honorary secretary of the station who had taken an active part.

These three services did not complete the work of the Dover lifeboat for that day, however. At seven-thirty the same evening the Sandgate coastguard reported that a yacht was drifting five miles south-east of Dover and the *Southern Africa* put to sea once more. It was still very rough with a south-westerly gale blowing and an ebb tide. The lifeboat found the yacht *Crevette* being towed by a cargo vessel, *Julia*, which was heading for Dover. Coxswain Walker thought it advisable to escort them and not long afterwards the towrope broke. He then took the yacht in tow with the lifeboat and returned to Dover. The *Julia*, which had four survivors from the *Crevette* on board, resumed her voyage to Antwerp.

Still on the same day, the Dungeness lifeboat was launched to the assistance of the motor vessel *Teeswood*, reported to be in difficulties four miles east of the ness. The *Charles Cooper Henderson* went sliding down the short slipway, over the wooden skids across the shingle and into the sea with a great burst of spray. As at Dover and Selsey the wind was blowing great guns, gusting up to 80 knots and creating a high, confused sea with flying spindrift. It was nearly 1300 when the lifeboat launched and about a quarter of an hour later the master of the *Teeswood* reported that the crew was taking to the boats. At this time the lifeboat was only a mile and a half away from the casualty but when she arrived on the scene the *Teeswood* had capsized.

The *B. P. Distributor* was standing by and had already picked up six survivors who had been clinging to floating wreckage. In the high waves, flying spray and rain it was extremely difficult to spot survivors from the lifeboat but the steamer directed them to the main body of the men in the water. All these men were in poor shape and unable to fend for themselves and the coxswain had to approach the group with great care to avoid injuring anyone. While the boat was in the middle of the group of survivors the propeller was fouled by wreckage. This was cleared by A. J. Oiller, the mechanic, who uncoupled the propeller shaft and by turning it by hand in the reverse direction, cleared the obstruction which was a piece of the mast of one of the *Teeswood*'s boats.

Also on the spot was an Italian liner of some 20,000 tons which was attempting to rescue a man in the water. A line was thrown to him but he was too weak to hold on and had to let go. The liner was now drifting down on to the lifeboat and Coxswain Tart had to go ahead and get out of her way quickly but his crew managed to rescue the man as they did so. One of the rescued was apparently drowned and a member of the lifeboat crew applied artificial respiration for an hour and a half, with both he and his patient being washed about the deck by the heavy seas.

At 1420 Coxswain Tart decided that there was no more that they could do and shaped a course for Littlestone to take advantage of any lee from Dungeness. The survivors were landed immediately on arrival at the station and taken to hospital by ambulances that were waiting.

On her way back to the station the lifeboat received a message that flares had been seen from a yacht off Dymchurch but Tart considered it imperative to land the men from the *Teeswood* first in view of their condition. As Dungeness has an open beach it is necessary to haul the lifeboat back on to her slipway and relaunch if she has to go off again and this was done in this instance. It was 1645 when she hit the water once more; again into a high, confused sea with a south-west wind of hurricane force.

The position of the casualty was given as one mile south of Dungeness and finding nothing here the lifeboat searched along the coast as far as Folkestone. The yacht in trouble was in fact the *Crevette* which was later towed into Dover by the *Southern Africa*, her crew having been rescued by the *Julia* which carried them on to Antwerp. Quite a lot of people must have ended up in places quite different from anything they had expected, that day!

The Dungeness boat returned once more to her station having been at sea for eight hours in terrifying weather but later that night another call came and at midnight she was careering down the ways to the sea again. The coastguard had reported a yacht in distress 15 miles south by east of Dungeness and with the wind now having veered a point or so the lifeboat had the sea nearly on the beam.

At 0119 on the morning of 30 July the lifeboat contacted the motor vessel *Dora* which had reported the yacht as being in distress. They said that they had lost sight of the yacht nearly three hours ago so Coxswain Tart asked the coastguard to arrange an air search at daylight. While doing this he was given a new position for the yacht as four miles south of Le Colbart lighthuoy. Arriving here at 0244 again they found nothing and commenced a search. Later it was reported that the yacht, *Right Royal*, was alongside the Dyck lightvessel and that the Calais and Dunkirk lifeboats were going to her assistance. After a somewhat frustrating night and having lost a lot of sleep they no doubt could have done with, the Dungeness crew were back at their station by 1130 on the Monday morning having spent 18 out of the last 24 hours at sea. Coxswain George Tart was awarded the bronze medal of the RNLI and A. J. Oiller and W. Thomas were accorded the Thanks on Vellum.

It has already been said that a medal for gallantry on this quite exceptional day was awarded as a result of a service carried out by a fishing boat. This in itself is not unique as the RNLI is empowered by its charter to reward any acts of heroism and lifesaving carried out by a boat from the shore. These are, in fact, known as 'Shore boat services'.

Still on the afternoon of 29 July, Mr Arthur Rouse, a Whitstable fisherman, was told that a dinghy was in difficulties off Tankerton. He went to the beach and through his binoculars could see a boat at anchor to leeward of the Street stones, a narrow shingle bank running out from the shore at right angles. At this time the dinghy was getting some shelter from the bank but it was clear that this would be lost when the tide rose. The coastguard had informed the Margate lifeboat station and the *North Foreland* (Civil Service No. 11) was launched but because of the distance she had to come it was doubted whether she could reach the dinghy in time.

Mr Rouse and a local boatbuilder, Mr Leslie Wood, decided to attempt a rescue with a local fishing boat, the *Audrey Russell* and the owner Mr Harold Rowden agreed, saying he would go with them. As soon as there was enough water in the harbour they put to sea. The south-westerly wind was blowing here with hurricane force but was, of course, off-shore. Even so there was a heavy sea on the beach and people had to crawl on their hands and knees in some places because of the powerful gusts. Fish boxes were said to be hurtling through the air, to add to the general unpleasantness.

Because of her draft, the *Audrey Russell* had to go round the seaward end of the Street stones and with the wind and sea on the starboard quarter she was in some danger of broaching-to, as she had no drogue. Rounding the end of the shingle bank the fishing boat had a very rough time in the broken water but Mr Rowden, who was at the tiller, came up alongside the dinghy in a bit of a lull and took off a woman and a man. The rescued pair had been fishing since early morning and had been caught completely unprepared for the sudden storm. With the dinghy in tow the *Audrey Russell* returned to Whitstable escorted part of the way by the Margate lifeboat which had arrived on the scene. For this rescue the bronze medal of the RNLI was awarded to Mr Rowden and the Thanks of the Institution on Vellum to Mr Rouse and Mr Wood.

Thirty-eight yachts were involved in the 52 launches made by lifeboats in that memorable 24 hours and no day before or since has emphasised so vividly the debt owed by yachtsmen to the lifeboat service.

Were it not for the necessity of providing a highly specialised rescue service in case aircraft may be forced to come down in the sea, the organisation for ordinary sea rescue would be far less extensive. Every aircraft route over every portion of the globe has rescue centres at key points with fixed wing aircraft and helicopters ready to take off at a moment's notice to search for a casualty. These aircraft are backed up by surface rescue vessels and in all constitute a world-wide rescue organisation of astonishing magnitude. This service is part of the International Civil Airlines Organisation and all countries operating civil aircraft contribute to it, generally by providing the rescue facilities over routes adjacent to their territories.

Happily, the history of civil aviation records very few instances of passenger aircraft coming down in the sea and the extensive organisation provided to deal with this eventuality is more often called upon to deal with marine accidents. In the wide stretches of open sea between the continents, far from land, the ICAO rescue service is likely to be the only help available to a vessel in distress, except for a chance ship in the vicinity.

Nearer at home, the occasional aircraft casualty at sea – in most cases a service plane – has meant long and often arduous searches in bad weather for both sea and air craft. Regrettably, a high proportion of these air casualties tend to be of a kind which leaves little hope of saving life; but the search must go on until every possible chance of success has gone. Occasionally though, a successful rescue is achieved, sometimes when least expected. One of these happened at Moelfre in Anglesey in 1943.

At 0015 on 21 October the coastguard reported an aircraft down in the sea off Dulas island, about three miles west of Moelfre. It was a dark night and the weather was bad with a strong southerly wind and a rough sea. The lifeboat launched at 0145.

As they cleared the land the lifeboat crew could see Very's lights from the ditched aircraft and when they arrived on the spot they found two fishing vessels standing by. These craft were unable to render assistance as the airmen had managed to get into their rubber dinghy which was now right in shore, being driven against the rocks with the survivors in danger of being washed out of it. The sea was too rough for the trawlers to lower their boats.

Coxswain John Matthews realised that there was no time to lose as the waves were washing right over the raft and breaking high on the rocky shore. Telling his crew to 'Hold on in case she strikes' he took the lifeboat inshore to where the dinghy was occasionally visible among the rocks. He had no idea what depth of water he had nor could he do much more than guess where any hidden rocks might be. Another hazard was the danger of running down the dinghy for although the boat's searchlight was used it was almost impossible to train it owing to the violent motion. In his subsequent report on this part of the rescue the lifeboat inspector wrote that it was rendered possible by a striking dispensation of Providence and great human skill and daring.

The lifeboat reached the airmen just in time as the second coxswain, lying on the foredeck, spotted the dinghy just as one of the airmen was washed out of it. All the survivors were exhausted and one of them had injured himself on the rocks. The second coxswain, who was the strong man of the crew, lifted the injured airman straight out of the water on to the deck of the lifeboat. Anyone who has ever had to get a man out of the water on to the deck of a small vessel will know just how difficult this is.

A line was then thrown to the three airmen still in the dinghy which they were able to secure. Matthews then somehow managed to go astern clear of the rocks, towing the dinghy into open water. Here the second coxswain again demonstrated his strength by lifting the three men aboard in turn, single handed!

Having thus successfully rescued the four airmen the Moelfre lifeboat returned to her station, towing the dinghy, and the survivors were landed and cared for. Coxswain John Matthews was later awarded the clasp to his silver medal, the second coxswain, Richard Evans, the bronze medal and the motor mechanic, Robert Williams, the clasp to his bronze medal.

At 2354 on the night of 26 April 1954 the coastguard informed the Eastbourne lifeboat station that two airmen were baling out of a Meteor aircraft two miles south-east of Beachy head. The lifeboat *Beryl Tollemache* was launched and searched the area in a rough sea and strong north-east wind. As in most cases of this sort it was very much like looking for a needle in a haystack and the type of service rarely attended by success. But on this occasion what might almost be considered a miracle happened; suddenly a rubber dinghy was sighted, close ahead. In it was one injured airman and he was carefully taken aboard and the search resumed for the other man.

The Hastings lifeboat had also launched and both boats made a wide search. The Eastbourne lifeboat picked up a parachute off Bexhill but no trace of the missing man was found. The rescued airman wrote a letter of thanks in which he said 'Up till then I had never thought about the work the lifeboat service does; but when the lifeboat picked me up after being afloat in my dinghy for two hours it was certainly the most welcome sight in the world.'

Chapter 10
Tankers in trouble

The possibility of having to attempt a rescue of the crew of an oil tanker on fire has for some considerable time exercised the minds of governments, shipowners and the rescue services. A great deal of thought and effort has gone into the work of organising special rescue facilities and in Britain regular exercises have been carried out to evaluate the arrangements, especially in ports with tanker terminals.

A number of ingenious devices and designs have been produced with a view to providing maximum protection from heat and flames for the rescue craft and their crews. The Japanese in particular have made a profound study of the problems involved and have built rescue craft said to be capable of operating in extreme conditions. The Dutch, too, have done a great deal of experimental work on the protection of craft in conditions of heat and burning oil and have established a number of interesting and important facts. One of these is that a fine continuous spray, as had been suggested to provide a screen, can easily be converted into steam by intense heat and become even more dangerous to personnel than the fire itself.

When a tanker is in collision the friction of two massive steel structures striking one another with enormous force invariably generates great heat and an oil or spirit cargo may well be set on fire, adding to the horror and confusion of the disaster. There have been a number of collisions involving tankers in the English channel, some involving loss of life, but probably not one that would be classed as a major disaster although there have been a number in other parts of the world including a very bad one recently in American waters.

There have of course been tanker casualties other than

those due to a collision round the coasts of Britain of which that of the *World Concord* in 1954 involved some fine rescue work by a British and an Irish lifeboat.

The *World Concord* was a tanker of 29,000 tons, registered in Liberia and bound in ballast from Liverpool to Syria. Early on the morning of 27 November 1954, during a storm of exceptional violence in the Irish sea, she broke in two just forward of the main superstructure, leaving the master and six men on the fore part and thirty-four men on the after part. She was of welded construction. The engines were in the after section and the propellers were still turning after the vessel split in two. The two parts of the ship began to drift apart immediately after the accident owing to the difference in size and windage and the fact that the propellers were turning. This of course was bound to complicate the work of rescue.

The first ship to respond to the SOS from the *World Concord* was the aircraft carrier *Illustrious*. She arrived in the vicinity of the casualty and stood by to assess the situation. Lowering a boat from a carrier is never a particularly easy operation and in the weather obtaining at the time it was probably almost impossible.

At this point the coastguard informed Dr Joseph Soar, honorary secretary of the St David's, Pembrokeshire, lifeboat station that the casualty and the carrier were some 10 mile north-west of the Smalls lighthouse and at 0648 the maroons summoning the crew were fired. But the lifeboat was not launched immediately as a number of conflicting messages arrived, first to say that the lifeboat was not needed and then later to say that she was. The matter was settled at 0800 when a mesage from *Illustrious* asking for a lifeboat was confirmed from the Commander-in-Chief, Plymouth. St David's lifeboat then launched with Coxswain Watts Williams at the wheel. At this time there was a moderate gale from the westward with a very rough sea and heavy rain squalls. Visibility was poor.

At 0915 *Illustrious* informed the lifeboat that *World Concord* was 15 miles north-north-west of the South Bishop lighthouse and the St David's boat reached the after part of the tanker at 1145. By this time the wind had increased to a fresh gale and had backed to the southward with a heavy sea and swell.

Coxswain Watts Williams, an outstanding seaman who had

served many years in sail, noted that the after portion of the tanker lay athwart the wind making conditions alongside extremely difficult. He decided to make a trial run to check the possibilities and after this asked for a rope ladder over the side of the tanker to be shifted forward of the superstructure, where there was still a short piece of deck left, just abaft where the break had occurred. This meant that a shorter length of ladder was necessary and also avoided some of the more broken water nearer the stern of the ship.

As soon as the ladder was in position the coxswain steered close alongside and as the lifeboat slowly passed a survivor descended and was quickly helped aboard. Thirty-four times this manoeuvre was repeated, only very skilful handling preventing serious damage to the lifeboat in the heavy seas alongside and from the jagged steel plates where the forward portion had broken away.

By this time the forward portion was out of sight and was drifting away rapidly to the northward. Watts Williams decided to return to St David's with the survivors leaving *Illustrious* to stand by the forward part of the tanker. Through increasingly deteriorating weather conditions the St David's boat made her way home, entering Ramsey sound from the north at about three o'clock to find that the strong current and steep seas on the slipway made re-housing very difficult and it was some time before the survivors could be landed.

Meanwhile the plight of the seven men on the fore end of the tanker had not been forgotten and the Rosslare lifeboat in southern Ireland had been asked to launch to their assistance as she was considered to be the best placed to effect a rescue. The weather was now extremely bad, so much so that the Fishguard–Rosslare steamer had taken twice as long as usual to make the crossing.

The Rosslare lifeboat *Douglas Hyde* left her mooring at 1550, soon after the St David's boat had arrived back at her station. Coxswain Dick Walsh in the Rosslare boat did not have a very easy task finding the fore end of the tanker in the severe conditions and poor visibility but shortly before six o'clock that evening a searchlight from *Illustrious* was sighted and further information was received from the tug *Turmoil* which was standing by to take one of the sections in tow.

Arrived at the tanker Coxswain Walsh had to decide

whether he should risk taking the men off in the dark or wait for daylight when in any case conditions might have improved. The broken section appeared to be riding quite safely and drifting northwards at about three-and-a-half knots. As the survivors were in no immediate danger he decided to stand by all night and if nothing untoward happened to attempt the rescue at daylight. The wind continued to increase and by midnight was approaching severe gale force from the west-south-west.

At 0830 Dick Walsh decided that the time had come to take off the survivors. The forward part of the tanker was running before wind and sea and listing about five degrees to port. Where the break had occurred there was an ugly line of jagged steel plates. There was a high, breaking sea.

After two trial runs the coxswain brought the lifeboat alongside the starboard side of the casualty about halfway along and well clear of the protruding steel plates. A rope ladder had been put over the side and by the use of the boat's engines he was able to keep her within reach of the ladder so that the seven men descended and were assisted swiftly into the lifeboat by her waiting crew. In spite of the rise and fall in the big seas and the grinding alongside the broken tanker the lifeboat only suffered superficial damage.

In view of the distance they had come north during the night and because of the need to get the survivors ashore, Dick Walsh decided to make for Holyhead as being nearer and a less arduous trip than the return to his own station. But he had underestimated the amount of drift during the night and would have overshot Holyhead had not an aircraft indicated the direction of the port, which the Rosslare boat reached at half past three that afternoon.

The breaking in two of an almost new tanker and the exciting rescue of her crew by a British and an Irish lifeboat of the RNLI caught the public imagination and was well covered by the press. The Rosslare crew were greeted by a brass band on their return and both Watts Williams and Dick Walsh were awarded the silver medal of the RNLI with bronze medals for the other members of the crews. This service still remains what may well be considered one of the most effective and efficiently executed rescues in the history of the RNLI, involving as it did lifeboats from both sides of the Irish sea.

The fate of the two parts of the tanker is also of some

interest. The fore part continued its hazardous journey north until it finally went ashore on the coast of Northern Ireland. The after part was eventually taken in tow and subsequently went back into service after the rebuilt fore part had been fitted to it in Antwerp.

The dreadful possibilities attendant on a tanker fire have been mentioned and the difficulties of rescuing men from a burning tanker, particularly in cases where escaping oil is on fire on the surface of the sea surrounding the vessel, can hardly be exaggerated. One of the less obvious hazards springs from lack of oxygen due to the huge amounts of air consumed by a major fire, so that suffocation is almost as great a danger as burning.

One of the worst tanker fires recorded happened in Japan in 1965 when the Norwegian vessel *Heimvard* hit a mooring dolphin and fractured a tank. The escaping oil caught fire and shortly afterwards a tank exploded, enveloping a large part of the ship in flames. It was nearly a month before the fire was brought under control and although ten people lost their lives it seems incredible that this figure was not much higher.

What might well have proved to be a major tanker disaster in British waters occurred in October 1970 when the 42,000 ton *Pacific Glory* collided with the 46,402 ton *Allegro* off the Isle of Wight. It happened at eight o'clock at night and the *Allegro* reported the collision by wireless saying that the damage was slight. In fact, the *Pacific Glory* was heavily on fire and residents in Ventnor and Shanklin could see the blaze and heard a number of explosions.

A German vessel, the *Nordwelle*, reported that she was picking up survivors, some of whom were swimming and some in boats. A later report said that out of a crew of 42, 29 had been saved and 13 were missing. As the ship concerned was foreign details of the actual rescue are unfortunately lacking but there can be little doubt that the escape from the burning vessel by survivors and possibly the rescue itself may well have been hazardous.

Tugs managed to get lines aboard the *Pacific Glory* and she was towed to a safe anchorage off Sandown, Isle of Wight, where she lay for some days before the fire was brought under control. She was then towed to Lyme Bay and anchored again off the Devon coast where she was anything but a welcome guest. In fact the spokesman for one local authority went so far as to say, 'We want her to get to hell out of here!' Later she was towed away and safely completed the voyage to Rotterdam where she was eventually repaired. It can only be said that things might have been much worse and no doubt certain lessons were learned from this incident which will be of value in any future case that may occur. It is a pity that details are lacking of what may not have been a great sea rescue but which was certainly a very valuable one to which a number of seamen must owe their lives.

Although not attended by loss of life as far as her crew was concerned the stranding of the 61,263 ton tanker *Torrey Canyon* on one of the reefs of the Seven Stones, between Land's End and the Scilly Isles, was the cause of more pollution and expensive effort than the *Pacific Glory* by a long way.

In daylight, having sighted the land and with every navigational aid at her command, the *Torrey Canyon* impaled her massive bulk on a pinnacle of rock from which all efforts failed to release her. The Seven Stones lightship had signalled, 'You are standing into danger,' in vain and within minutes of the impact oil began to gush through a 500 feet gash in the giant hull. Ten of her 18 tanks had been pierced and from these her cargo of 118,000 tons of oil began to pollute the surrounding sea. It was the beginning of the biggest oil slick ever and one which brought into action a host of people and thousands of gallons of detergent. The damage to wild life was extensive and many beaches were covered with a thick, tarry-looking deposit which put an end to any thoughts of sand castles and buckets and spades for a long time. The clearing up cost was enormous.

The weather was fine and initially the crew elected to remain on board but on the following day, a Sunday, the Isles of Scilly lifeboat took off 22 men without much difficulty. One man fell into the sea but was hauled aboard the lifeboat and possibly because of this incident the remaining nine members of the crew decided to remain where they were. In any case they appear to have lost their confidence in marine craft because when a helicopter appeared they left quite happily. This left Captain Pastrengo Rigrotti and three officers on board together with two salvage men from the Dutch tug *Utrecht*.

By this time the many craft employed to deal with the oil slick were hard at work but only with moderate success as within two days the menacing black sheet of oil had grown to a monstrous 18 miles long and two miles wide. At the same time the salvage team was working at top pressure to refloat the ship, using every modern device available. One man was killed when compressed air being pumped into the hull blew off a hatch.

A week after the stranding the wind changed and began to sweep the oil towards the Cornish coast. It soon increased to gale force which sent in a heavy sea which before long broke the tanker in two. And still oil poured out of her.

By this time the whole British nation was conscious of what was happening between the Isles of Scilly and the Cornish coast and a lot of people were saying, 'But there are now hundreds of the super-tankers – this could happen every day!' The government was well aware of the magnitude of the problem and members of the cabinet visited the scene to see for themselves, holding a meeting at nearby Culdrose naval air station. As a result troops were called in to assist in clearing the beaches and at Marazion people turned out to neutralise the oil by pouring detergent on it from watering cans.

Still the *Torrey Canyon* continued its vindictive pollution as oil poured steadily out of the broken tanks. Aircraft were called in to bomb the wreck in the hope that the remaining oil would catch fire and burn out where it lay but the success of this operation was minimal. Other aircraft dropped 5,000 gallons of a petrol-paraffin mixture and soon an enormous fire was raging with a pillar of smoke thousands of feet high which could be seen from Land's End. The effectiveness of these very expensive operations was open to doubt but at least people knew that every effort was being made to reduce the area of eventual pollution as far as possible. Nothing like this had ever happened on the coast of Britain before and there was some insistence that steps must be taken to prevent it happening again.

By now the oil had spread from Hartland point on the north Devon coast right round Cornwall to Start point in south Devon but by the end of March it was decided that the *Torrey Canyon* had shed its last drop of oil and the detergent fleet went home. The army remained to continue the depressing and dirty job of cleaning the beaches. Not a great rescue as far as the lifeboat service was concerned but a new and important type of casualty which must needs be recorded.

The dangers of collision in which tankers are involved has already been stressed. In the case of the *Pacific Glory* lives were lost and a fire on board took many hours to subdue. In January 1971 the Panamanian registered *Texaco Carribean* of 13,604 tons exploded after a collision with the Peruvian ship *Paracas* off Folkestone. The force of the explosion ripped away the bow section which sank at once but the after part drifted for some hours before finally sinking.

The explosion was felt twenty miles away and along the coast from Hythe to Dover windows were shattered as were some as far inland as Tenterden. Eight men, including the master were found to be missing when a roll call was taken and 22 survivors, still dazed from their experiences were picked up by the Norwegian ship *Bravagos* and transferred to Dover lifeboat which landed them at Dover where they were taken to hospital. The other vessel concerned, the *Paracas*, was taken in tow to Hamburg with a badly damaged bow.

Once more, what could have been a disaster of the first magnitude with possibly the loss of most of the crews of both ships involved, resulted in the majority of the crew of the exploding tanker being saved. How they escaped seems little short of miraculous but perhaps it will not always be so.